F. Sava J. Grozdanović / Prof. Aleksandar Marinković / Prof. Lazar J. Grozdanović

VOLLEYBALL
for
Boys & Girls

An **ABC** for Coaches and Young Players

Meyer & Meyer Sport

Original title: Odbojka ABC
® 2001, prof. Aleksander Marinković

British Library Cataloguing in Publication Data
A catalogue record for this book is available from the British Library

Sava J. Grozdanović / Aleksandar M. Marinković / Lazar J. Grozdanović:
Volleyball for Boys and Girls
– Oxford: Meyer & Meyer Sport (UK) Ltd., 2003 –
ISBN 1-84126-126-2

© 2003 by Meyer & Meyer Sport (UK) Ltd.
Aachen, Adelaide, Auckland, Budapest, Graz, Johannesburg, Miami,
Olten (CH), Oxford, Singapore, Toronto
Member of the World
Sports Publishers' Association (WSPA)
www.w-s-p-a.org

Printed and bound: Finidr s. r. o., Český Těšín
ISBN 1-84126-126-2
E-Mail: verlag@m-m-sports.com
www.m-m-sports.com

CONTENTS

CHAPTER 4

CHAPTER 5

CHAPTER 6

FOREWORD

In the last couple of years a high level of results in the sport of volleyball have demanded a wider and more complex basis for selection in terms of basic skills, the physical conditioning as well as the complex psychological preparation of volleyball players. This extremely high level can only be attained through many years of planned and systematic learning of techniques (i.e. early specialization), which must be planned on the scientific basis of modern education and training. Many years of systematic and complex preparation of young players are necessary in order to prepare them for physical and psychological efforts, demanded by high level of training and competition. It is important to bear in mind that this youngest age (6-14 years of age) is the best for acquiring such skills. It is the age in which the greatest biological growth occurs and the development of technique, speed and agility also takes place at this time. It is also important to remember that the way of working and living (school, nutrition, fun, sleep, etc.), are all factors that have a great impact on achieving the highest results.

The authors of this book about volleyball are brothers Sava and Lazar Grozdanović and Prof. Aleksandar Marinković, who have distilled their years of valuable experience into this book. Teachers and Coaches working with young people who want to dedicate themselves to volleyball will find in this book the latest practical experiences and up to the minute information. Finally, it is important to emphasize that one of the authors, Laza Grozdanović, used to be a Selector of the Yugoslav National Team and that he significantly contributed to the development of the sport in this country, for which we are grateful, and wish to express our thanks to him.

Vladimir (Vanja) Grbić and Nikola Grbić

CHAPTER 1

Your Students May Be Interested
in the Historical Development of Volleyball

Below it is described in twenty-four simple illustrated points

1. Playing a ball with hands in the ancient times – Playing a ball with both hands was well known from the ancient times. The only issue was whether it was played with a small or a large ball (tennis or volleyball), for example the inflated belly of an animal that was being hit, or with a ball filled with some material that was being caught. All games with ball in which it was hit or caught with hands, generally originate from Pan Ancient or Ancient Games. These ball games were very popular, especially among young women. In the illustration above, such a game between two Roman girls was shown on a mosaic*. Volleyball acquired its sports character by the end of the 18th century.

  * Piazza Armerina, villa Erculia

2. America, the homeland of volleyball – Volleyball is one of the games from the group of youngest sports created in the United States at the end of 19th century. In the United States, back in 1895, main emphasis was on American football, baseball, tennis and track and fields.

3. William Morgan, father of volleyball – During the winter 1895, conditioning trainer William Morgan (1870-1942) in the city of Holyoke, was concerned about how to organize a conditioning training for the players of baseball, rugby and basketball.

4. Volleyball was created in a gym – What he did was to put a tennis net across the middle of the gym. The height of the net was 198 cm. 6-7 players on each side of the net tried to throw the inner rubber ball of the basketball over the net. Morgan called this game a "mintonet".

5. The first public match in Holyoke – In 1896, Morgan was invited by the UMSA (Christian Youth Society) to demonstrate his new game. In a new gym, beside the city of Holyoke, in front of numerous people, two teams composed of five players each played this game for the first time. Captain of one team was the Mayor himself, James Kerry (known as the fat one), and of the other, Lynch, chief of the Fire Brigade.

6. The name "volleyball" given by Prof. Alfred Halstead – The same year, 1896, looking at this game, Prof. Alfred Halstead named it "volleyball", meaning in English, the ball that flies. The name remained the same throughout the century.

7. The first description of the game in the magazine "Physical Education" – This specialized sports magazine published the first description of the game with the following words:
...Volleyball is a game that can be well played in the gym as well as in the open. Number of players is not limited. The ball is being thrown over the net until it falls to the ground...

8. Volleyball developed from fusion of two sports – Volleyball developed from a mixture of tennis and handball (or better *hazena*). The net was borrowed from tennis, as well as the rule for two attempts of serves.

Two periods of development of volleyball

The first period starts with its creation, in which the rules of the game are being determined, and the game itself is spread all over the world.

Volleyball had a big success in neighboring countries from the very beginning.

The second period starts from 1947, when FIVB, International Volleyball Federation was founded, and lasts to this very day.

9. A game without direct contact with the opponent – During the game, there is no direct contact with the opponent. The game itself is not aggressive; it may be played in a lighthearted manner and as such has become very popular. The bladder of a basketball, which was used at the time, proved to be unsuitable due to its size, and was soon reduced to a ball, which was smaller and softer. The height of the net was also raised to 243 cm for men.

10. Expansion of volleyball from its homeland (USA) into other countries – The sport of volleyball very quickly became popular in the country of origin, firstly, as an excellent conditioning game for other sports in wintertime, and later on as a sport in its own right. From the United States it spread fast in neighboring countries (Mexico, Cuba, Panama, Argentina, Brazil), and then on to other continents, especially Asia, where it became very popular.

11. Volleyball in Pan Asian Games – Volleyball occupied an important part in these Games, in which China, Philippines, Indonesia, Burma and other countries participated. A fact that proves the popularity of this sport is that in the period from 1913 until 1934, 10 such tournaments were organized.

12. Volleyball in Europe – Volleyball was brought to Europe by American soldiers during the World War I (1914), namely to England. In the homeland of football, this game did not attract much interest; in fact it was ignored and indeed even mocked.

13. France, pioneer of European volleyball – However, the real popularity and mass interest in volleyball took place in France, primarily in schools and universities. Thousands of fans developed an interest in this exciting sport. Volleyball, as well as being played indoors, in sports halls, was more and more turned to being played outdoors. From 1938, the first championships started attracting large interest of spectators.

14. Volleyball in Czechoslovakia – the first National Volleyball Federation for Men was founded in Czechoslovakia in 1924, and for Women in 1931. The famous Czech School of Volleyball was renowned for the quality of individual technique.

15. Volleyball in the USSR – Volleyball was then introduced in USSR where it has been played since 1919. Volleyball was also played in the first Spartak Games - Spartakiade in 1928 (competition based on the principles of the Olympic Games). The USSR has been very successful in European and World Championships, the Olympic Games, and other events.

16. From Poland, volleyball spread to Baltic countries – In Poland, volleyball has been played since 1920. Already in 1923, the first Competition Rules were printed. From Poland, volleyball spread to the Baltic countries (Lithuania, Estonia, Latvia).

17. Berlin, 1936, Reduction of Rules – In Berlin, 1936, during the Olympic Games, the International Volleyball Commission revised the American competition rules, which were valid until then. A metric system was introduced for measuring. For example, the net was fixed to 243 cm for men and 224 cm for women.

18. Paris 1947, the year the FIVB (Fédération Internationale de Volley-Ball) was founded including 14 countries – This was the first international federation in charge of volleyball and included: Italy, Holland, Belgium, Yugoslavia, Romania, Hungary, Portugal, USA, Brazil, Uruguay, and Egypt.

19. Olympic Games Tokyo, 1964 – Volleyball appeared for the first time on the program of the Olympic Games in Tokyo 1964. Besides the Olympic Games, the most important volleyball competitions held were: World Championships for Men in Rome 1948, and World Championships for Women in Prague 1948.

20. Leading world nations in volleyball – Nowadays, the best volleyball is being played in the following countries: Russia, Italy, Yugoslavia, USA, Holland, and Cuba. Excellent volleyball is also played in Czech Republic, Bulgaria, Spain, Romania, Brazil, and other countries.

21. New Rules of the Game – By introducing new Rules of the Game (hitting the ball with feet allowed, number of points raised to 25, points are counted as in tie-break ...), gave a new, fast rhythm to the game and made it more interesting for the spectators.

22. Ruben Acosta promotes volleyball – When Dr. Ruben Acosta became President of the International Volleyball Federation, significant changes in the quality of volleyball were made. Rules were changed, new competitions were organized, and as a result the interest of spectators for volleyball has grown. As regards the number of member federations (216), the International Volleyball Federation is the first in the world (followed by basketball, track and fields and football).

23. "Beach Volley" – Recently, more and more attention is drawn to this kind of volleyball competition that is played on sandy beaches in nice and warm weather. Teams are usually composed of two players on each side. "Beach Volley" has become an Olympic sport since the Olympic Games in Atlanta, 1996.

24. Volleyball, sport of the future and the young – Volleyball, being a sport played with minimum equipment, whether indoors or outdoors, presents a sport of the future. Its recreation role is emphasized, aiming to improve health status.

Chapter 2

Points for the Attention of Teachers and Coaches

Before starting to work on the techniques, skills and tactics of the game teacher/coaches should check the following aspects of students' individual development.

Correct Body Posture

It is good to see a young person who stands correctly upright. When standing, sitting and walking, such an individual holds his head and body straight, while the shoulders are pushed slightly back. The posture of the body depends on each individual. The correct posture of the body is not something that is inherited; it is something that is learned and once learned it should be preserved, from childhood through to old age. In children of the age about which this book is written, the skeleton has not yet been fully formed. The spine is still flexible and not very strong, and weak and undeveloped muscles can cause incorrect body posture that leads to distortion and deformation of the spine. With the passage of time the gristle in the spine slowly ossifies, i.e. it becomes bone, and if the spine is deformed at this stage it's too late to do anything about it. Incorrect standing, besides not looking good, also causes numerous complications related to the spinal cord, as well as the function of many organs close by. These are the reasons why, if the young person wishes to be completely healthy, it is important to make an effort to stand up straight. When standing and sitting, the head and body must be straight, with the shoulders pushed slightly back. Correct body posture can be acquired and maintained through some exercises, which should be performed each day, for example, during the PE lesson.

Volleyball everywhere – for everyone

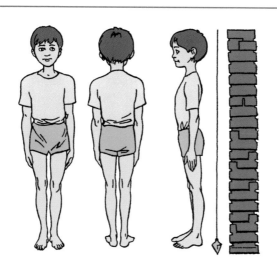

Fig. 2.1: The correct standing position

Fig. 2.2: Correct sitting position   *Fig. 2.3: Not like this!*

Walking

In order to practise volleyball, it is important to first learn how to walk correctly. Everyone knows how to walk, but few people actually walk correctly.

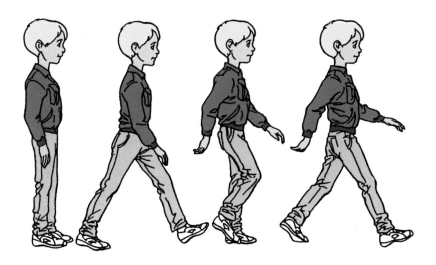

Fig. 2.4: Correct walking position

The person who walks correctly is generally slower to tire, and hence may be more receptive to guidance. When walking, the head should be lifted straight, so that the eyes are directed forward and not downward. The shoulders drawn slightly back, arms stretched out and moving front-back (left arm - right foot, and vice versa). Almost the whole surface of the foot is placed on the ground, with slight emphasis on the heel. The feet are parallel when walking. The step is vigorous and it is important to breathe freely and deeply. In fact if the students thinks about the proud walk of an animal such as the stag it may help to get the idea across to them.

Sun, Water and Air, Activities in the Open Air

In order to develop physically correctly, it is important that as much time as possible should be spent in unpolluted air, in the sun, and whenever possible the student should drink as much water as possible. These three things (clean air, sunlight and water) are vital for the life of every individual, and especially for the development of young people. It is, therefore recommended that the students should spend at least 2-3 hours per day where possible outside in the fresh air. For this reason they should attempt to plan their day in such a way that after school there is enough time to spend in the open air, relaxing and playing. With the help of friends, and parents the day should be planned such that day and night are balanced. During the day it is important that the students should attempt to strike a balance between the activities of learning, eating, playing and resting.

Fig. 2.5: The stag

Correct Starting Positions for Exercises

Before starting to exercise it is important to adopt an appropriate position that will help the student to carry out the movement correctly.

See Fig. 2.6, which gives 11 ideas of the correct starting positions from which to initiate exercises.

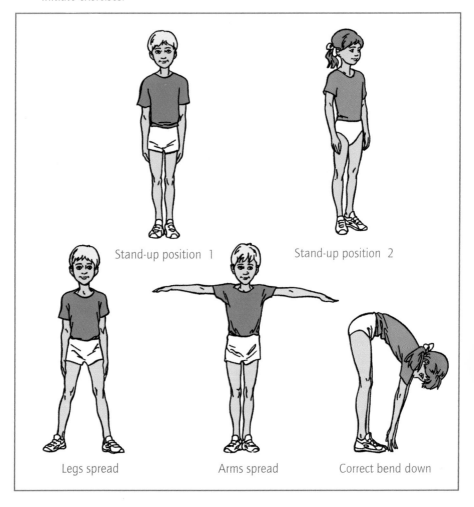

Stand-up position 1

Stand-up position 2

Legs spread

Arms spread

Correct bend down

Squat – with hands in front

Sitting position

Kneeling position

Kneeling support

Lying position on back

Lying position on front

Fig. 2.6: Correct starting positions

Learning to Run Correctly

The whole world over, one of the most popular challenges among boys and girls is – "let's see who can run the fastest". It is possible to run almost anywhere: in fields, through woods, in the streets, around the house, and on a football field. There's no greater joy than feeling the fresh airflow around the body and the blood running vigorously through the veins. Running is fun and is pleasant, but running has also become a sport in which people want to develop great speed. Running is the oldest competitive sport in the world. It is important to be aware that running is indeed very important for other sports as well. If the student masters running in a correct way, then that can help him/her to become a good volleyball, football, basketball or tennis player. Running is also important in all children's games.

It is therefore necessary to master running, first slow running ("jogging"), then fast sprint and finally middle distance running (for example "cross- country").

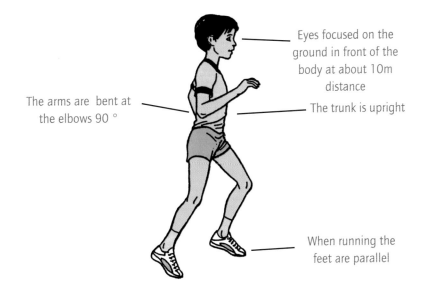

Eyes focused on the ground in front of the body at about 10m distance

The arms are bent at the elbows 90 °

The trunk is upright

When running the feet are parallel

Fig. 2.7: *Technique for slow running (jogging)*

The trunk is slightly bent forward

Hands swing alternately in front of the body to a point the level with shoulders

As the hand swings back it is level with the hip

The breathing should be carefully monitored

land on the front part of the foot

It is important to try and run on the balls of the feet.

Fig. 2.8: Technique for long distance running used during warm up

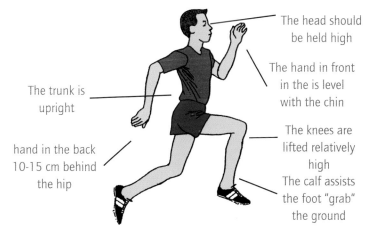

The head should be held high

The hand in front in the is level with the chin

The trunk is upright

The knees are lifted relatively high

hand in the back 10-15 cm behind the hip

The calf assists the foot "grab" the ground

Fig. 2.9: Technique for fast running – sprinting

When running fast it is very important to do exercises for the feet.

The next illustrations show detailed instructions for different types of running (trotting, sprint, middle distance running).

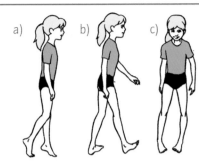

Free fast walking

Walking exercises:
a) on tip toes, b) on heels, c) on the outer ridge of feet

"Charlie" walking,
legs astride

Running with knees
raised high

Short step movement
"toes-heel"

Hands movement on
the spot

"Toes-heel" on the sport
using intensive arm work

Walking with thread of
string around the neck

Running with legs straight

Running kicking the heels towards the bottom

Running with relaxed arms

Exercise on the spot for "scraping" step

Coach (or a friend) holds the runner with one arm (running on the spot), then lets him go suddenly

Running uphill – slow or fast

Fig. 2.10: Examples of running drills

"Warm-up" before Exercise – "Cool-down" afterwards

Warm-up has great importance not only prior to competition but also during training. Warming-up improves the different aspects of the body and prepares it for the required effort when training. Additionally, it creates conditions for maximum performance during competition.

Fig. 2.11: Slow running (jogging) and stretching exercises are 'a must' during both training and competition. The same goes for "cooling-down" process – for example running after the match (barefoot if possible).

Research has shown that after the warm-up results were better, that the exercises were performed with a greater accuracy, preciseness, greater strength and skill. During the warm-up, the following physiological changes take place: oxidation initiates a change in blood composition, and the functional state of the cardio-vascular and respiratory systems change, etc. An example might be that a runner starts an 800m race without previous warm-up, he would run to the end not reaching his full potential. The warm-up is a complex of specifically chosen exercises that should be performed in order to prepare the body for the work. Following warm-up the body temperature raises causing a decrease of tiredness. A warm-up session has two parts, a general or introduction part and the second, more specific, in accordance with the needs of different sport disciplines.

The session usually starts with slow running – jogging, together with walking. Then come general exercises, worked out in two segments.

The first is done in a very gentle and relaxed manner, with a small amplitude and intensity of movement. In the second segment, the individual works with greater amplitude of movements and in an intensified manner. Between exercises it is necessary to relax the muscles, one method to do this is to run gently using short intervals. Each movement should be repeated 8-12 times.

In the second part of the warm-up, it is necessary to introduce a couple of specific exercises for each specific discipline. The warm-up session is then finished with some few slightly speeded up exercises .

After the students have finished the practice session or training – it is necessary to "cool down". This is usually done in only a couple of minutes, where there is a clear association between slow running and stretching exercises. "Cooling-down" or "running-out" helps to improve the oxidation of the waste products that accumulate during physical work.

It is important to emphasize that a good warm-up before a training or competition and a good "cooling-down" can significantly prevent injuries.

Volleyball everywhere – for everyone

Making forward and backward circles with arms

Turning the trunk to right and left

Bending deep forward

Kick forward and backward

Making circles with the whole body

Bending deep forward with legs spread apart

Lying on the floor, straighten the leg and bring to sides, from left to right and back

Lying on the back, the scissors

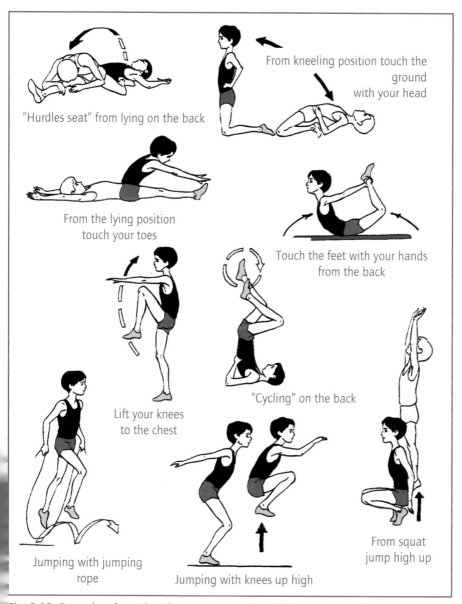

Fig. 2.12: *Examples of exercises that are commonly used in warm-up sessions*

How to Develop your Students' Basic Physical Abilities?

Very often, when people speak about sport, they are talking about physical abilities. These include all the different features of the human organism that enable him or her to be quick and have strength, agility and endurance. Physical abilities are the building blocks of an active life: they may enable the student to be in good health, good form, to increase their work rate, and if necessary, to have the ability to fight off infection. We are talking here about those basic physical abilities that are the building blocks of physical condition, namely: speed, strength, stamina and flexibility.

Here are some explanations about them and how they develop.

Fig. 2.13: *There goes your cap! Girls can do it faster!*

SPEED – is an ability to make one simple or several complex, or several associated movements for the shortest possible period of time. Also, it is an ability to react to a certain stimuli (for example, a sprint start), in the fastest possible way. Speed develops when young, from 7 until 14-16 years of age. Many pages in this book are dedicated to the development of speed, and teacher/coaches are advised to study it well.

Fig. 2.14: The student should be strong to carry a 'friend' across a stream, so her feet don't get wet

STRENGTH – is an ability that enables the body to perform some movement or some work connected with the muscle effort, for example, lift an object (arm strength), push some object (a car – strength of the arms and legs – or the whole body), or to climb up (the stairs – from one leg to the other). Strength depends on the muscle fibers. The more massive the muscle, the greater the strength. Strength develops faster than speed, but it also decays when not used and training ceases. One should be careful when applying strength exercises in younger ages. All exercises should be suitable for the age of the individual. At a young age the most important aspect of strength is the strength of the muscles of the legs, back, arms, abdomen, back and shoulders.

Fig. 2.15: Walking and long running are the best exercises to develop endurance!

ENDURANCE – is an ability to perform some activities for a long period of time (slow running, cycling, rowing, slow swimming, etc.). It is necessary to pay attention to endurance, whether the actual participant takes part in sports or not. It is a good characteristic to have when young, but it also comes in handy at older age. Exercises for developing endurance are simple: they are all those activities that take some time – for example for young people aged between 7-14 they must work for at least 4 minutes to achieve any measure of endurance. The movement may be shorter, but it must be repeated several times, for example drills that are repeated with short breaks in series (for example, running 100 meters for 10-15 times).

Fig 2.16: Picking something up with straight knees

FLEXIBILITY – means the ability of the joints and elasticity of muscles. This is of great importance in all aspects of our everyday lives, and especially important when mastering techniques in certain sports. Young people show greater ability to improve this elasticity, while at old age this ability significantly decreases. That is why improvement of this ability relates predominantly to young people.

Exercises for improving flexibility can be practised alone, with or without apparatus. The aim of all these exercises is to increase the amplitude of the movements in all major joints in our body. These exercises are performed after a good warm-up, before or after a training session. Each exercise should be repeated 10-15 times.

AGILITY – is an ability to perform complex movements in order to move some parts of the body, the whole body, or certain objects from one place to another, and ways to overcome some obstacles in complex situations. Agility is developed from very early age. In boys and girls of senior grades in primary school, agility is developed through basic sports and games, and then, with a higher level of sports technique, depending on what sports discipline is chosen.

Agility can be very well developed through the use of acrobatics.

Fig. 2.17: Do a forward or backward roll!

Control Health and General Physical Well-being

Before starting to train for volleyball, it is necessary to perform a medical health check on each candidate, or at least, to take into consideration their school health records. It is important not to forget that only absolutely healthy children should start with sports training. Health checks should be made twice a year.

In order to evaluate general physical form, it is necessary to carry out testing. Before testing, one should warm-up and the results obtained must always be registered. This kind of testing (together with the medical health control), should also be done twice a year.

One should also bear in mind that these are only standard parameters, and not some final marks or evaluation whether someone is fit and able to train volleyball or not!

Volleyball everywhere – for everyone

Tab. 2.1: Suggested framework of standards of fitness relative to age

Control Exercises	7-9 yrs		10-11 yrs		12-14 yrs	
	Girls	Boys	Girls	Boys	Girls	Boys
1. 30 m sprint (standing start) The runner starts running at his own command. Time is measured from his first move.	5,4 s and better	5,5 s and better	5,3 s and better	5,1 s and better	5,1 s and better	4,9 s and better
2. Forward jump The mark of the heel is measured.	1.35 m and better	1.40 m and better	1.55 m and better	1.70 m and better	1.70 m and better	1.80 m and better
3. Hang-ups From arms stretched position raise the chin to the bar.				2-3	1-3	2-4
4. Push-ups when lying	1-2		2-5	3-6	4-6	5-9
5. Raising up leg to 90 degrees When hanging on a bar, branch pull legs up to horizontal position.	1-2		3-4	5-7	4-6	6-8
6. Bridge or split	Without bending over, girls do split and boys do the bridge (stretched arms).					
7. Bend forward to bench the ground	Girls are supposed to touch the ground with palms and the boys with finger tips, without bending the knees.					
8. Throwing the medicine ball over the head backwards 7-11 group throws 2 kg ball 12-14 group, a 4 kg ball	3,00 m and better	3,60 m and better	4,20 m and better	4,70 m and better	4,50 m and better	5,50 m and better

The Importance of Developing Speed while Young

Exercises for Developing Speed – Imitation of Positions and Movements of Various Animals

During the practice sessions, movements of the whole body as well as the positions taken before the beginning of each exercise are very important. The student should try to take the positions and perform the in the correct way. If they follow the presented material, they will have the chance to experience the exercises with the correct position.

The objective of this type of work is to ensure that the students imitate the positions and posture of specific animals, until a whistle is blown (this can be done without the use of a whistle but it is entirely up to as the teacher/coach). The students should then sprint quickly (5-30 m). This drill should be repeated two or three times. A 2-3 minute break between each attempt.

Fig 2.18: Imitation of various animals

It is sufficient for them to do three to four exercises during one practice.

1. **PROUD DEER** – try to walk like a deer, with his antlers proudly held high;

2. **GIRAFFE** – emulate giraffe with its neck high above, browsing on leaves;

3. **ROOSTER** – stand on one foot, with one hand on the head, fingers spread like crest on rooster's head;

4. **COILED SNAKE** – sitting, pull the knees to the chest and coil like a snake;

5. **WALK LIKE AN ELEPHANT** – make all the moves like when an elephant walks. If necessary the students should be shown a video or even visit the zoo and watch carefully how elephant moves;

6. **STRETCHED OUT SNAKE** – lay on the front and stretch out as much as possible;

7. **MONKEY** – imitate a monkey when sitting on the ground. Ask if they have seen such as wildlife programmes on television?

8. **CURLED HEDGEHOG** – take a position of a hedgehog when he is completely curled up for defence;

9. **FISH** – lay on the front and curl up as the fish in the illustration. Look how the fish wriggles when it jumps out of the water;

The above listed exercises are just a few ideas of how it is possible to get young people to move the whole body. Also, visit the zoo or look at videos and note how some of the animals move! Try finding some others that are not included in this list.

Before running, remember to warm up well.

Use examples of exercises provided in Fig. 2.12.

Developing Speed with Racing in Different Ways
(Children from 5-7 years of age)

Youth, as was mentioned above, is the best time to develop speed.

Speed is a determining factor in modern sport and success in many sports greatly depends on speed. In general, between the ages of 6-8, speed can be developed with exercises and simple games. The students can learn them themselves, or better with the help of their parents, teachers or older friends. We have presented here two "circles" of simple exercises, helping them to develop speed.

1-7 starting positions for exercises for speed development – imitation of postures and movements of animals and people

Fig. 2.19: Different free distance running

Different free distance running, which is limited to 5-30 meters, with previously determined distance, is run in various ways, such as are:

1. **"LIKE A FLYING BIRD"** – the student "swings" his arms up and down, like a stork flying;

2. **RUNNING UPHILL** – the body is slightly bent forward in running. Swing the arms powerfully beside the body;

3. **"HORSE GALLOP"** – when running like this, the student "grabs" each step in front of them. They are supposed to imitate the movement of the horse's front legs in the horse races (or like the ones pulling chariots). Study this movement well, either on TV or video;

4. **INDIAN RITUAL "DANCING"** – the students are asked to imagine that they are doing an Indian ritual-dance calling for the rain. The whole body is in movement. This can be easily seen in Western movies on TV or in the cinema;

5. **RUNNING AROUND** – this is best done around low bushes or trees;

6. **RUNNING DOWNHILL** – the students run down a small downhill, relatively flat (to avoid any injuries), with a lot of free space to run;

7. **"RUNNING FIGHTING"** – while running the students are asked to imitate movements of a boxer in ring, step dance, different blows (uppercut, hook, etc.). Imitation goes for the footwork as well, running around the ring and similar.

NOTE: On a previously determined distance (5-30 meters) each running practice is to be done in series of two. The first with slower movements and the second with faster and stronger movements. Between exercises take a 2-3 minute break. It is sufficient to do 3-4 exercises.

Please Note This Important Advice!

If the student wants his or her approach to playing volleyball to have the greatest possible effect, beside the instructions just mentioned, it is advisable to consider some other very important advice:

THE COACH – The role of the teacher/coach in this educational and training process with young people is of utmost importance. The teacher/coach, in his work with young players, must help to develop some positive features: courage, persistence, initiative, and discipline. Beside, these and in accordance with the students innate ability he should help improve the psychomotor abilities (speed, strength, agility, endurance, etc.), such that they can fully acquire all knowledge and skill, necessary for obtaining the best possible results in volleyball. The coach will help with his advice, it is also very important to remember that young people see in coach the role model for their own sports life. He should always be ready to help his students in every difficult moment they pass through.

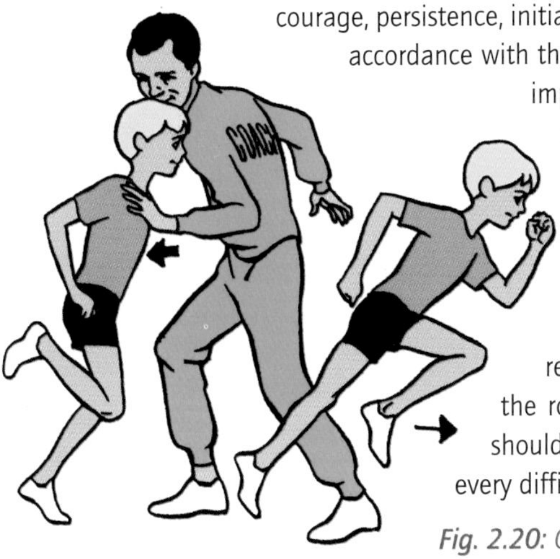

Fig. 2.20: Coach

A QUESTION OF HYGIENE – During exercises, muscles need the power that is provided by nutrition and oxygen. That is why it is so important that practice takes place as often as possible in the open, in the fresh air, or in an air-conditioned clean hall, or, where viable, in the students own home. Dust, smoke and fumes from the exhaust systems should be avoided whenever possible.

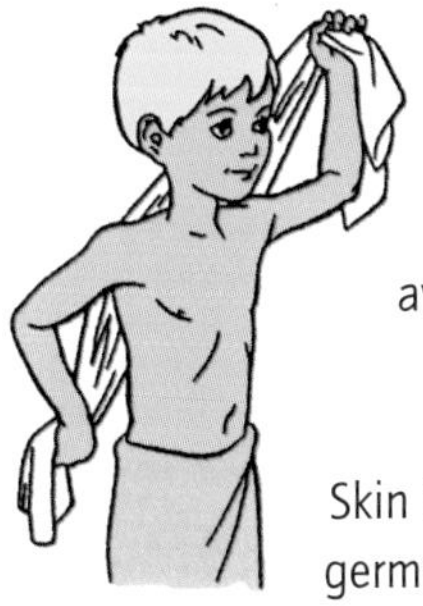

Fig. 2.21: A question of hygiene

Skin is the body's protective envelope, shielding inner organs from various germs, and from external influence, helping regulate body temperature, and eliminating all waste products from the body. In regular conditions, we eliminate through our skin one liter of sweat and a few grams of salt every day. In case of intensive physical exercise, the body perspires a lot more, and if one considers the secretion of seborrheic glands, dirt and micro organisms gathering on the skin, it is understandable why we should shower with lukewarm water after each training session.

TRAINING AND COMPETITION EQUIPMENT – Sports outfit should be light, comfortable and airy, and should only be worn once during training or competition. The students 'kit' should be washed, cleaned and aired after each single use. A sports outfit (shirt, shorts, training-suit, socks, etc.) should be made of 100% cotton, if possible. A tracksuit is a good idea when warming up, especially when the days get cold.

Sports shoes (trainers) must protect the feet from injury, dirt and cold. That is why sports shoes must be roomy enough, warm enough, enabling the player to move well. Cramped shoes hurt feet (sore feet, blisters), pressing the blood vessels. Be very careful about the outfits and sports shoes in various climates and during different weather conditions (autumn, winter, rain, etc.). The choice of outfit and footwear should be made together with the coach or teacher. The equipment is only intended for training and competitions, and it is personal. For reasons of hygiene, it is to be learnt by everyone!

Equipment for training and competition is strictly personal:

1 Competition uniform for boys and girls
2 Shorts
3 Socks (stockings)
4 Sneakers
5 Reserve socks
6 Soap
7 Towel
8 Bag

Fig. 2.22: Equipment for training and competitions

IMPORTANT FOR GIRLS – between girls and boys, there are many significant differences, and it is normal and necessary for different activities and the way in which they are performed see Fig. 2.23. Girls cannot compete together with boys in volleyball as for one thing the net is positioned lower for the girls.

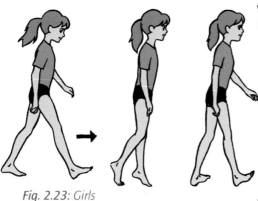

Volleyball, and especially jumps, are very favorable for the development of girls. It is however necessary to be careful with older girls during their menstrual cycle. If it goes normally it is acceptable to practise in this period, but not as intensively as normal. In any case, it is not advisable to go for long runs or walks, or exaggerate using exercises for the abdominals. With reasonable practise the player will adjust easily and this will not trouble them either now or in later years and in sports.

Fig. 2.23: Girls

Strength exercises should be carried out only in agreement with you, the teacher/coach!

NUTRITION – Food is fuel – Live organisms constantly use energy. This power or energy is necessary for each activity, especially for sport activities. Food does not only provide energy for living beings, it enables all normal functions of their bodies, the regeneration of cells, creation of tissues and organs, in fact growth and development.

On the following pages there are suggestions for daily meals for young volleyball players.

Fig. 2.24: Nutrition

Correct Diet For Young Volleyball Players

In order to develop properly, beside sport activities in the open, in the sun and with the help of water and other procedures of personal hygiene, adequate nutrition is extremely important. The body partly uses food that is introduced into it as a construction material (proteins, for example), building muscle fibers, bones and other parts of the body, while the rest is used to make all that function (fats and sugar). Young players develop only when there is a balance between food that is taken in and that which is used by the body. That is why the diet for students of this age should be plentiful and varied. In order to grow, it is important to have regular, plentiful and varied meals (good quality). That means three meals a day (breakfast, lunch and dinner), every day at the same time, but it would also be good if the player would drink a glass of milk, juice or have a fruit between the meals, in the morning and in the afternoon. All meals should be composed, beside bread and pasta, first of all of vegetables, fruit, meat, eggs, fish, milk and dairy (cheese, cream, yogurt, sour milk), and different salads. Cakes, creams, chocolates and other sweets and soft drinks are also food for players of this age, but only if taken in limited quantities and only after main meals. On page 48 there is a suggested menu.

NOTE: In order to have all sessions of both training and competitions carried out in a proper way, it is necessary to take the time to digest all the food eaten. This is why we propose that the last meal is finished at least two hours before training and three hours before competition.

Tab. 2.2: Vitamins useful during more intensive trainings

VITAMINS USEFUL DURING MORE INTENSIVE TRAININGS			B6
PHYSICAL ACTIVITY	VITAMIN	FOOD	B12
SPEED	**B** GROUP	Dark bread, meat, fish, fruit, vegetables, eggs, milk, yeast	
STRENGTH	**E**	Nuts (walnut, hazel-nut, almond, Indian nuts), fish-oil, green peas	E
ENDURANCE	**C**	Fresh fruit and vegetables: lemon, orange, kiwi, strawberry, apple, dog-rose berry, pepper, sauerkraut	C

Tab. 2.3: Suggested menu for young Volleyball players

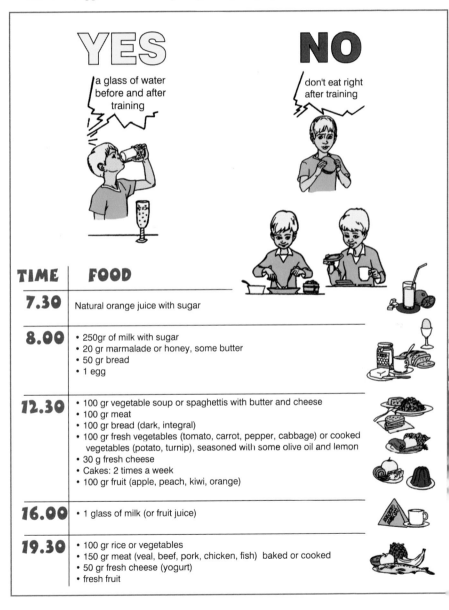

TIME	FOOD
7.30	Natural orange juice with sugar
8.00	• 250gr of milk with sugar • 20 gr marmalade or honey, some butter • 50 gr bread • 1 egg
12.30	• 100 gr vegetable soup or spaghettis with butter and cheese • 100 gr meat • 100 gr bread (dark, integral) • 100 gr fresh vegetables (tomato, carrot, pepper, cabbage) or cooked vegetables (potato, turnip), seasoned with some olive oil and lemon • 30 g fresh cheese • Cakes: 2 times a week • 100 gr fruit (apple, peach, kiwi, orange)
16.00	• 1 glass of milk (or fruit juice)
19.30	• 100 gr rice or vegetables • 150 gr meat (veal, beef, pork, chicken, fish) baked or cooked • 50 gr fresh cheese (yogurt) • fresh fruit

YES — a glass of water before and after training

NO — don't eat right after training

Illustrations Without Words

Describe the working day of a student from getting up in the morning to going to bed at night.

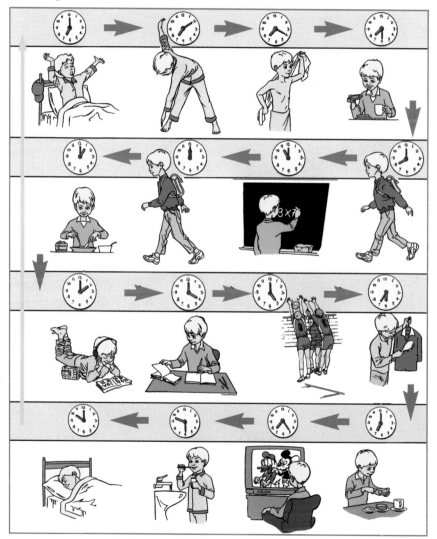

Fig. 2.25: Describe the working day of a student

CHAPTER 3

The ABC Approach To Training Young Volleyball Players

What Does the **ABC** of Volleyball Mean?

The fact that training for young players should correspond to their biological development has already been mentioned. First of all, the physical preparation should be well planned, engaging the whole of the body. It is important to emphasise that if a teacher is working with the young people it should be possible to implement such a programme during the students' PE lessons.

In modern volleyball it is accepted that the player is supposed to reach his/her maximum technical and competitive abilities as an adult. However, by the judicious use of certain specific volleyball training at an earlier age some young players may achieve their maximum capacity earlier in life. However, care must be taken in order to avoid great dips in performance that can happen when the young person is not mentally strong enough to deal with serious competition. Having said this it is still true to say that the best performances in sport comes after the young player reaches full maturity as a grown-up athlete.

The **ABC** method is one that is systematically planned and directed and based on concentric circles. (See Fig. 3.1) The work itself is expressed as a percentage (%), in which three basic components are emphasized (**A**, **B**, **C**), where **A** presents working on individual technique, **B** is physical conditioning, and **C** is tactics, training and competitions.
    In other words these 3 components added together should produce the result of excellent volleyball players

A (technique) + **B** (conditioning) + **C** (tactics, training, competitions) = RESULT

In order to make the "concentric circles" method more acceptable, it will be of benefit to look at the main features of the theory applied to the youngest age groups where the coach may find an answer that may be if interest.

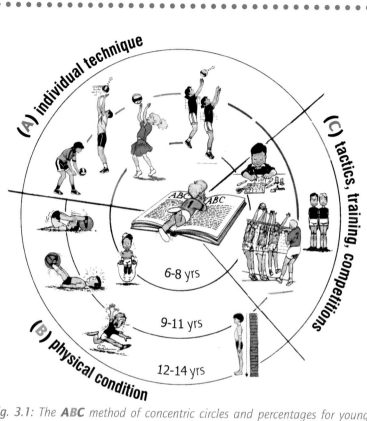

*Fig. 3.1: The **ABC** method of concentric circles and percentages for young volleyball players*

This method means that the teacher/coach can work simultaneously on the different aspects of the game but spending different percentages of time on each aspect as illustrated below:

Table 3.1: The concentric circles method (%)

Age	(A) individual technique	(B) physical condition	(C) tactics, training, competitions
6-8 yrs	25%	70%	5%
9-12 yrs	40%	50%	10%
12-14 yrs	40%	40%	20%

As a result of this type of training the Yugoslav volleyball team won the gold medal in Australia 2000, and became Olympic Champions, joining the football team who did the same in 1960, water-polo (1968, 1984 and 1988), and basketball players (1980).

The Main Features of Working with Young Players of Age 6-8

In the previous developmental stage (under 7 years of age), the child developed his imagination, usually keeping himself entertained. Later, when in school, together with his or her friends, the child learns through simple elements of work (games, running, simple jumps and throws), through simple tasks that must be well thought out.

The basic task is to make children perform as many different movements as possible, it is important to stress that whether they perform them correctly or not is of secondary importance. With this age group, exercises should always be presented in the form of a game.

The Main Features of Working with Young Players of Age 9-11

It is a characteristic for this age that the body is more unified in its development, speed and agility are developed, and the child masters movements in a more efficient manner. As children of this age express greater and more permanent ability to remember things, it is easier to demonstrate certain elements of the technique, with the prospect of seeing them performed correctly and more precisely.

The Main Features of Working with Young Players of Age 12-14

It is in this age group that the most obvious changes happen, not only in physical but also in the mental development. When a child gains height fast, this can lead to extension of the tubular bones and muscles and the child takes on a 'skinny' and elongated look, which results in the slower development of strength muscles. Changes in bodily structure influence the functions of all organs. The heart muscle grows as it works harder, being forced to provide greater quantities of blood to the tissues. This results in a subsequent raise in blood pressure, as the development of cardio-vascular system falls behind the heart growth. Increases in the secretion of the glands brings sudden changes in psychological state of the child, such that at this period they may express greater sensitivity and irritation.

In training young players, especially in the first years of development, it is necessary to use a wide variety of exercises. Each exercise must, in its character and form, correspond to the needs of modern volleyball.

It is what we set out to do in preparing to write this book, i.e. each technical element is followed by a corresponding set of exercises.

The **ABC** Approach to Teaching Volleyball

In order to be successful in playing volleyball, it is necessary for each young player to prepare his abilities (speed, strength, stamina, elasticity and agility), in accordance with his age and specific ability level. It is necessary that he masters all elements of technique (handling the ball), and all necessary tactical elements of volleyball, which make up the technique of a game.

Technique is the most important part of the game of volleyball and, is composed mostly of groups of elements, such as: passing, digging, spiking and blocking the ball. That is why many exercises and games used during training contain tasks that are presented in such a way that they train all these elements in a combined way, i.e. the way the player will have to use them in the game. Training young players, differs from the more or less already known and accepted methods such as analytical or progressive parts (looking at different specific phases of the game), or complex (looking at whole elements).

Summing up the approach and work in our so-called "Volleyball Schools" for young players, the central place is occupied by the "game method", even though all others are equally represented, this is done with the objective to correct any given mistakes and to present the students with a realistic picture of what might be expected to be met with when they are playing the full game.

The "game method" or whole-part-whole method is a method in which several elements are put together, in such a way as to simulate the real game or part of the game.

As with in any other method, the "game method" uses a basic order which is as follows:

1. Create a clear image of the required technique. This may be done through a demonstration performed by an eminent player or the coach. Videotape may also be used, as can such as demonstration posters and in fact any other means of communicating the visual image of the technique to be learnt.

2. It is important to pair off the players according to their technical ability. Players should work in pairs or in groups, depending on availability of space, balls, etc.

3. Players are divided in groups according to their knowledge. This means constant movement between groups in order to avoid promising players being slowed down by their less good peers.

4. There should be a systematic increase of intensity of exercises depending on the method of teaching being used.

The "game method" is performed in three different phases:

Phase I: Technical elements should be taught in an available space, so long as the players reach a reasonable degree of mastery of certain programme elements.

Phase II: Elements should now be transferred to a volleyball court (leading up to the game). At this stage the coach must insist on the correct use of space, meaning, for example, that orientation in attack is the opponent's part of the court, and on this part of the court, players are to take the most convenient position in order to prevent the opponent to perform his game – the defence tactics.

Phase III: The teacher/coach presents a simulation of one part or the whole game.

When teaching volleyball to young children it is important to ensure that the information made available to them is absolutely up to date, is professionally presented and that they can perform the set tasks, namely that the tasks are adapted to their age and ability level. When choosing exercises for teaching children, one should always take care that each movement is composed of something basic and something special, making it unique from other movements. For example to coach a cover attack from the back-court players who move forward from the back court, this is standard work, but if the coach adds to the end if this move a dive retrieve at the end of the first phase of the movement from, for example a fed ball or a rebounded smashed ball then he would have added something special/specific. It is also important to choose those movements that will take them to the goal the fastest way.

It is also important to stress that in order to give the players the best possible visual image of the technique or skill to be mastered there must be a good well produced demonstration; a bad demonstration must be avoided at all costs. It is very useful to show a movie, a videotape, poster, demonstration poster, or similar. The demonstration of whatever is being shown must be seen by everyone. It is good, at least for the beginner and for the young players, to base their technical model on a good, famous player (i.e. a "role model"). Technique must be adopted as soon as possible, because the sooner it is done the better, as in this way it is slower to fade from the student's memory.

The process of learning a technique can also be taught by using the video-motor approach to the technique. If using this method it is important to ensure that the students give their full attention to the process, i.e. they should be fully engaged in a psychological way.

If using this method it would be very useful for children to see themselves on video. The movements should be analyzed using real time speed, and also in slow-motion which could be extremely useful ("frame by frame"), and could speed up the process of learning.

Educational Facilities Required Using the "Ideo-motor" Method of Educating Young **ABC** Volleyball Players

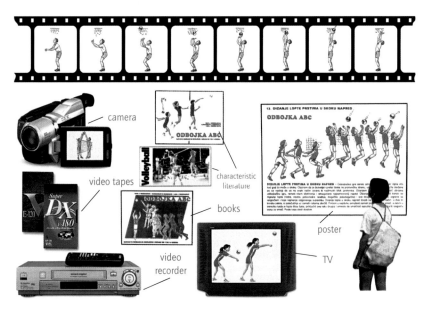

Fig. 3.2: The basic equipment

It has been proved that 85% of information received by the central nervous system (c. N. S.) is received through the "visual field" (eyes)

Fig 3.3: "Eye-moving muscles"

"Eye-moving muscles"

- **A** – eye muscles enabling the movement upward-sideways
- **B** – eye muscles lifting eyelid
- **C** – eye muscles enabling the movement upward-straight
- **D** – movements outward-straight
- **E** – movements downward-straight
- **F** – movement downward-sideways
- **G** – optic nerve

Exercises for Improving the Eyesight

As the eyesight is so vital in all sport it is important to try to improve each individuals eyesight in line with their innate ability. The result will certainly contribute to the eyesight of those who need it, and their number throughout sport is large, for example shooters, field invasive and other games players, track and field athletes etc. Improved eyesight also helps the players to gain in confidence and become more outgoing; so that introducing them in this programme is completely justified. Exercises should be performed in every available moment and space.

It is especially useful to practice them in the open for example on a hillside – in the outdoors , for example on the top of a hill where it is possible to find enough objects in the far distance to observe. The character of these exercises is no doubt useful and numerous documents confirm it. In the illustration (see Fig. 3.4) it is possible to see how this "eye moving machine" functions.

Exercise 1. The exercise is to be performed in the following way:

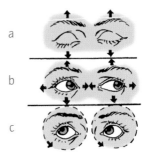

a   Abruptly close and open your eyes widely. Repeat 5-6 times with a rest interval of 30 seconds.

b   Look upward, downward, straight, without moving your head.

c   Circle with your eyes (imaginary circle), downward, straight, upward, left and right, and then reverse the circle.

Exercises B and C should be done with opened and closed eyes. Repeat every exercise 3-5 times with an interval of 1-2 minutes.

Exercise 2. Starting position: Direct your eyes to the top of your forefinger, some 20-30 cm away from your eyes (1) The look fixed on your finger, should be transferred to some other far away object (tree, house, mountains), 200-800 meters away (2). Repeat this several times.

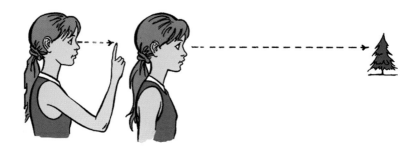

Exercise 3. Lightly massage lids over closed eyes (1) with the tips of your forefingers (2). This results in an increased blood supply to the area massaged.

Exercise 4. From the position on your illustration a (eyes opened as wide as possible), suddenly close your eyes and shut them tightly (as in illustration b), and then open them widely again)

a   b

Exercise 5. Starting position: Look towards your forefinger (a) and fix your fingertip. Move your finger to the right and follow it, without moving your head. (b) Return your finger to the starting position. Repeat the exercise several times. The same should be done with your other hand in opposite direction.

Exercise 6. Hold your index finger raised at about 20 cms on front of your face (a). And focus on the tip of your forefinger. Cover your left eye with the your palm and only view your finger with one eye (b). Repeat viewing with your left eye only (c).

Exercise 7. With the opposing finger extended about 20 cms ahead of your face move your finger towards your eyes while continuing to look at it. (a) Slowly move your forefinger towards your eyes while looking constantly at the tip of your finger. Return your forefinger to the original starting position and repeat several times

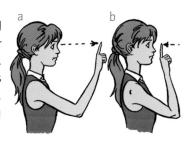

CHAPTER 4

Volleyball Technique

In this section of the book the teacher/coach is presented with a visual and written analysis of a specific technique followed by diagrammatic examples of the types of taining required by the players.

Figs. 4.1 and 4.2 show clearly the essential elements of volleyball. For example, in Fig. 4.1 numbers a-d illustrate the position and orientation of the hands, while e and f show very clearly the contact points of the ball on the fingers.

Fig. 4.2 simulates almost perfectly the main shots of the game, viz the dig the dive and the set, plus the 4 possible positions of the hands. So these two Figures set the scene and it is now down to the reader, to use this book to find out much more about how these, plus other techniques and tactics, are used in the game

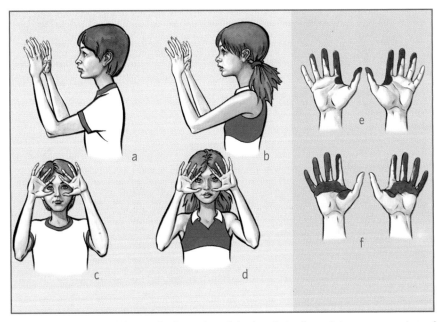

Fig. 4.1: The position and orientation of the hands (a-d), and the contact points of the ball on the fingers (e-f)

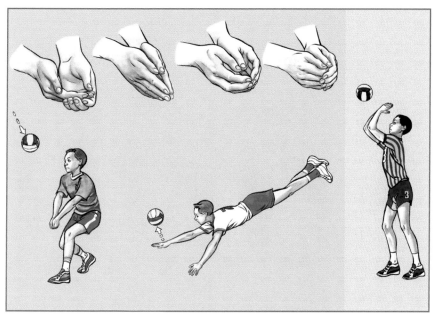

Fig. 4.2: The main shots of the game, plus the 4 possible positions of the hands

Volleyball everywhere – for everyone

Playing the Ball with the Fingers

| 1 | 2 | 3 | 4 | 5 | 6 | 7 |

Fig. 4.3: Playing the ball with the fingers

When playing the ball with the fingers, feet are straddled, somewhat bent knees, one leg slightly forward. The body is bent slightly forward. Arms are raised to the height of the forehead, bent at elbows and not too wide apart. Hands are at some 20 cm away from the head (forehead). The fingers are spread, with the wrist a little bent backwards. When rebounding - passing the ball, the fingers taking the most impact are the forefinger, middle finger and the thumb, with the ring-finger and the little finger taking the least. The ball must not fall on the palms. Upon the contact with the ball, all parts of the body spring up, legs, torso, arms, hands, fingers (illustrations 5, 6, and 7).

Playing the ball with the fingers enables a shorter passage of the ball from one player to the other ("setter"). The two ways of playing the ball, the one with the fingers of both hands and the one with the forearms, "the dig", are the basics in a volleyball game. The player must strive to transform this rebounding into passing, meaning that it is not sufficient to receive the ball sending it somewhere, it is important not to "handle" it.

Playing the Ball with the Fingers of Both Hands (Setting) while Falling

Fig. 4.4: Playing the ball with the fingers of both hands (setting) while falling

For this technique of playing the ball, it is necessary that the player takes a correct position with the body towards the ball, wherever it may be. In order to pass it well, he must take a position with a view of the place of where he is intending to send it. When directing the ball, the player should be turned towards the player to whom he is passing.

Having passed the ball he should roll to the side (illustrations 7 and 8). The head of the player should always be behind the ball and under it. The weight of the body is shifted to the leg that corresponds to the side from which the ball is passed (illustrations 4, 5, and 6).

In the past this element was not often used, but in the current game in the last period, players who are fit use it very often, due to the fact that it is possible to obtain greater accuracy, and that the possibilities for an attack are more varied and it is generally considered more efficient.

Passing the Ball with Both Hands in a Jump Set

1　　2　　3　　4　　5　　6　　7　　8　　9

Fig. 4.5: Passing the ball with both hands in a jump set

In modern volleyball, this technique is frequently used, because it improves precision and increases the speed of the game.

The position of a setter is the most responsible in the team. The "setting" itself is the perfect form of passing the ball. That is why it is so important to pay great attention to teaching this element. In performing this element of technique, one can easily spot skills of a future good "setter". In this technique, one leg is positioned a little bit in front of the other and is a little bent at the knee.

Exercises For Playing The Ball
(Rebounding And Passing – "Volleyball Gymnastics 1")

Fig. 4.6: Exercises 1-5

The Muscels Used when Receiving the Ball with the Fingers

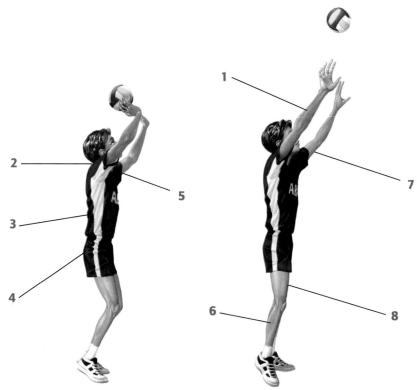

Fig. 4.7: The muscels used when receiving the ball with the fingers

1	MM – finger extenders
2	MM – neck extenders
3	Back muscles (Back extenders)
4	Gluteus – bottom muscle (hip extender)
5	Arm raisers (forward – back)
6	Gastrocnemius –triceps muscle below the knee (foot extender)
7	Brachial triceps – muscle of the forearm (forearm extender)
8	Thigh quadriceps (extends the leg below the knee)

Exercises to Increase Strength and Flexibility

1

5

making "circles"
with arms

2
(2/3/7)

exercises for the shoulder area

3
(8)

jump from squat
with a sand bag
(1-3 kg)

6

5   (2/5)

(3/5/6)

7

(3/4)

lifting the bar with
weights (10-25 kg)

lifting legs backward

lifting your hips with the help of your partner

8
(1/5/7)

9
(1/5/7/8)

throwing the medicine
ball forward

walking on hands

10
(8)

11

squats - jumps
(with a medicine ball)

squats with partner
on your back (not so
heavy, under 30 kg
partner)
(4/8)

4   (1/4/7)

walking on hands with the help
of your partner

Fig. 4.8: Exercises 1-11

Note: The numbers match the respective muscle workout.

Exercises for Playing the Ball with the Fingers

Fig. 4.9: *Exercises 1-6*

Note: The numbers on the lines of movement signify the order of performing the exercises.

Exercises for Rebounding and Passing the Ball

Fig. 4.10: Exercises 1-5

Exercises for Rebounding and Passing the Ball with the fingers: "Volleyball Gymnastics 2"

Fig. 4.11: Exercises 1-4

Note: The numbers on the lines of movement signify the order of performing the exercises.

Rebounding the Ball with a "Dig"

Fig. 4.12: *Rebounding the ball with a "dig"*

In both demonstration posters it is clear that the position of legs and body are almost the same as in rebounding and passing the ball with the fingers of both hands. Legs are more apart but the leg in front is not so far away. The hands are lowered (nos. 2 and 3) and completely extended, and are joined together so that they make one whole. The hands can be folded together in several ways, while two have the greatest effect (nos. 1 and 2). The player reaches for the ball, following it with the whole body, until the very last position (nos. 6, 7, and 8). This way of rebounding – passing the ball is applied mostly when the player receives a service, in cases of some medium and strongly spiked balls.

Modern volleyball has accepted this way of rebounding and passing the ball as the basic, and the most important, and it is very much used, almost in 90% of the cases. Even though it looks quite easy to carry out, it is the most difficult element, because, beside a good and correct technique it is essential to have a good concentration, feeling of space around, reflex, calmness, precision and speed.

Hitting the Ball – High "Dig"

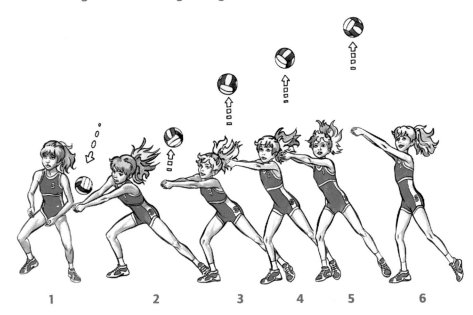

Fig. 4.13: High "dig"

When playing on defense the player has to receive spikes; here the high "dig" is very frequently used. Spikes are normally hit very hard, or served so that they reach the player at chest height and to the side, so it is very important to use this shot to counter such a ball.

The high "dig" differs from the basic "dig" in two ways – position of legs and the position of the arms. In the high "dig" it is important to step out with one foot to the side to which the ball falls.

Another thing is, when the player holds the hands to form the "dig" position, one hand must be held a little higher, so that the "dig" does not present a flat surface, from which this spike or hard ball just rebounds and drops to the ground. All other principles regarding the basic "dig" apply here as well.

Rebounding the Ball with a "Dig" while Falling

Fig. 4.14: "Dig" while falling

The same principles apply to this skill as to the basic "dig". The only difference is that the ball usually falls low, the player must step out to receive it to the left or to the right, depending on where the ball falls. As these are very low balls, the player is obliged to step out, the position in which one leg is bent in the knee, and the other is stretched out to the side.

After receiving the ball and passing it on, the player leans and then rolls backwards. In this element, the ball is always lower than the head, and the whole body is under the ball and in the position to receive it with a "dig".

In the game, this element is often used as it is much simpler and easier than playing the ball with fingers. Usually it is more used for rebounding than for passing (simpler element).

Muscles Used in Playing the Ball with a "Dig"

Fig. 4.15: Muscles used in playing the ball with a "dig"

Hand Extensors

1	Neck extensors
2	Thigh quadriceps (extends the leg below the knee)
3	Back muscles (back extensors)
4	Deltoid muscle (shoulder raisers)
5	Brachial triceps (forearm extensors)
6	Abdominal muscles

Exercises to Develop Strength and Flexibility

1

(2/4/5/7)

Circles with the torso

2

(4)

"Scissors" lying on the stomach

3

(1/6)

Hand stand with the help of a partner

4

(6)

Lifting a barbell (5-20 kg)

5

(7)

Exercises for the abdominal muscles

7

(2-5)

6

(2-6)

Stand up from squat position, holding a medicine ball

8

(1/7)

Sway around with a sand bag (2-5 kg)

Lift a barbell (10-25 kg)

Fig. 4.16: Exercises 1-8

Note: The numbers match the respective muscle workout.

Exercises for Passing the Ball with a "Dig"

Fig. 4.17: Exercises 1-5

Note: The numbers on the lines of movement signify the order of performing the exercises.

Receiving the Ball with One Hand Sideways

Fig. 4.18: *Receiving the ball with one hand sideways*

This technique is used for receiving balls that arrive at the player unexpectedly, and fall too close or too far away for the player to respond with the standard "dig" or to receive the ball with the fingers.

The ones that are too close, actually hit the block and are falling unexpectedly. In the second case the ball is far away and the player has to get it in a hurry. Therefore, as the standard "dig" is not possible, the player hits the ball with one hand. In order to do this the player performs this technique using the inner boarder of the forearm, or the hand or even the shoulder.

If the ball arrives on the right the player steps onto the left foot, the leg of which is straightened. If the player has to sprint to get to the ball, it is permissible to use the hand or fist to play the shot.

Receiving the Ball with One Hand while Falling Sideways

Fig. 4.19: Receiving the ball with one hand while falling sideways

In the game of volleyball some balls can only be reached by falling in order to reach them, these are generally short, low balls. If the player has to receive the ball with one hand he usually steps out to the side with the right foot if the ball falls to the right and the left if it is vice versa. The arm and hand are extended maximally in an effort to reach the ball, and the ball is hit with either the fore arm or the hand or fist. The ball should go as high as possible in order to help the team to pass it on. Due to this step to the side, the player is bound to take another step or two and a roll forward. Receiving the ball with one hand to the side is often used in a game. It happens in cases of all tipped or spiked balls from the block, and players have to receive them like this, while falling sideways.This element is extremely attractive and resembles the movement if a soccer goalkeeper, it is often used for receiving the ball, but rarely for a controlled pass.

Playing the Ball with One Hand while Falling – the "Dive"

Fig. 4.20: The "dive"

This is a typical technique for playing the ball, and is the kind of play that is used when the ball is far and ahead of players. It often happens when the ball falls behind the block and there is no other way of bringing it successfully into play. The player should be in a very low position (see no. 1), from which he springs from one leg forward (see nos. 2, 3), after the ball. At the moment he plays the ball, the player is in horizontal position (nos. 5, 6). Playing is done with one hand, the upper part of the hand (no. 5), and the player tries to bring the other hand into play such that he falls to the ground with his weight on both hands. He hits the ground with both hands, followed by the chest and then the whole body. The "dive" is the most attractive and the most difficult technique used in volleyball. It is used mainly to "withdraw" balls from behind the block.

N.B. While teaching this element, great care should be taken and start from soft falls (on the mattress).

The "Sliding Dive"

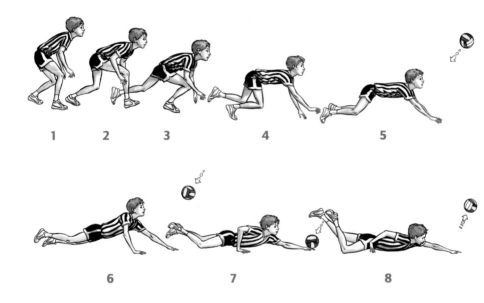

Fig. 4.21: "Sliding dive"

This differs from the classical "dive" in which, to reach it when it's out of his reach, the player takes two steps and then throws himself from above after the ball, and is also a way to "save" the ball. With the "sliding dive" a player should succeed in saving the balls that are relatively close to him and suddenly fall to the ground. In these cases the player is not able to make any steps, but he must throw himself from a very low position straight to the ground and literally "dive". The body is almost parallel to the ground, and the player, with his arm stretched out "dives" to save the ball, which it would be impossible to receive otherwise. The ball is struck by the upper part of the hand, and rebounds into the air, from where his team mates can pass it on.

Exercises for Rebounding and Passing the Ball ("Volleyball Gymnastics 3")

Fig. 4.22: Exercises 1-4

Note: The numbers on the lines of movement signify the order of performing the exercise.

Muscles Used in Playing the Ball in a "Dive"

Fig 4.23: Muscles used in playing the ball in a "dive"

1 Neck extensors
2 Gluteus – bottom muscle (hip extensor)
3 Thigh quadriceps (extends the leg below the knee)
4 Gastrocnemius – triceps muscle below the knee (foot extender)
5 Biceps femoris (flexes the leg below the knee and extends the hip joint)
6 Finger extenders
7 Arm lifting muscles (forward, back)
8 Brachial triceps (forearm extensors)
9 Back muscles (back extensors)

Exercises to Develop Strength and Flexibility

1 (7)
2 (2/9)
Moving arms forward - backward

Lifting the upper part of the body together with legs held with arms

3 (7)
Extension of shoulder area

4 (3/4)
Start with "falling" forward

5 (2)
Lifting hips against resistance

6 (3/9)
Lifting something while astride (medicine ball)

7 (4)
Lifting yourself on tiptoes

8 (3/4/7)
Exercises with jumping rope

9 (3/4/7)
Jumping up with knees held up high

10 (1-9)
Roll over a box horse

Fig. 4.24: Exercises 1-10

Note: The numbers relate to each different muscle group defined on the left.

Playing the Ball with the Foot

Fig. 4.25: Playing the ball with the foot

In order to promote the game and make it more attractive, the newest changes of the rules allow players to play the ball with all parts of the body, even foot. There are two cases in which this technique is most often used.

The first is when the ball falls very close to the net or just right to it, often, these are balls resulting from a failed block. The player must react quickly then, and reach with hands to receive the ball. It is more efficient and easier to do the same with the foot. If the ball is hit too far over the court, the player has to run to catch such a ball. In this case the only solution is to play the ball with the foot. This is done with the left or the right foot, over the head and high into the court. The hit is actually done as in soccer, with the upper part of the foot (see nos. 6 and 7).

Setting the Ball with the Fingers of Both Hands without Jumping

| 1 | 2 | 3 | 4 | 5 | 6 | 7 |

Fig. 4.26: Setting the ball with the fingers of both hands without jumping

In setting the ball the position of the fingers, arms, legs and the whole body is just the same as in passing, but it must be very accurate, because this technique is usually the "second" ball, softer and passed by a team player. When setting the ball, it is very important to think tactically, because in a volleyball team, the role of the setter is the most responsible one. Setting the ball without a jump forward demands that the whole body works in synch: the legs are set a little apart, the knees are bent, the hands in their final phase are parallel and as stretched out as possible. The body follows through the whole action. There also must be a precision element to this technique in that such a set ball is designed to be passed to the team player with great care. The same goes for all set balls. This kind of setting, without the jump, is not often used in modern volleyball, especially when the ball passed is high and close to the net.

Setting the Ball Backward without Jumping

1   2   3   4   5   6   7   8

Fig. 4.27: Setting the ball backward without jumping

As was mentioned previously, the perfect form of passing the ball is setting. In this case, setting backward is purely a setting technique. Today it is usually performed beside the net or towards the net, also from the net to team player for an attack on the opposition spiker. With this technique, as with all other techniques for setting, beside the perfect skill in using fingers, the player must have a perfect tactical thinking. The position of the body is similar to setting the ball forward. Legs are a little bent and somewhat apart, fingers are spread out, hands at the level of the face and the player tries to receive the ball in front of his forehead. When the player has the ball, with his whole body, from legs, up across the body and with his arms stretched, sets the ball with his hands, following it closely with his eyes. The position of the setter in the team is the most responsible one, because he takes part in all phases of the game and connects the whole team. As a rule, the players that are setters must be in perfect physical and mental condition.

Setting the Ball with the Fingers while Jumping Forward

| 1 | 2 | 3 | 4 | 5 | 6 | 7 | 8 | 9 |

Fig. 4.28: Setting the ball with the fingers while jumping forward

The game of volleyball today demands the setting to be done wherever it is possible to do it, but lays emphasis on using a jump. As blocking is permitted in the opponent's space, the role of the setter is even more difficult as he constantly tries to trick and overpower the block of the opponent team. By setting the ball with a jump, the setter speeds up the game, disturbs the rhythm of blockers and enables a multitude of different attacks. It is possible to set all balls (low, high, semi-high, middle, long, semi-long) using a jump plus all other balls that have been practiced with another team player, and that create the most problems for the opposition. Setting the ball using a jump is performed in the following way: in a two-three steps approach, the player adopts a semi-squat position and jumps up with hands in the air. He feints in the air as if to play a spike, and when the ball is close to the hands, he joins the other hand and instead of spiking, with the hands stretched out he passes the ball to a team player for a spike. After that he returns to the ground.

Setting the Ball Using a Jump Backward

1	2	3	4	5	6	7	8

Fig. 4.29: Setting the ball using a jump backward

Everything said previously regarding setting the ball from a jump using a forward facing position goes for this technique as well. Preparation for the jump, position of the body, hands, legs and the jump itself until the ball is in the hands of the setter are the same. From that moment, he is supposed to estimate which teammate is in the best position for a spike against the opponent team. So, the ball should be sent to the best estimated position. He must take into account who is the player that passes the best, or which combination can "trick" the block. Most frequently, the player sets the ball to the diagonal – spiker at about 3 meters from the center line. Here also, as it is obvious on nos. 4, 5, and 6, that in setting all parts of the body function together. Hands in the jump direct the ball, arms are extended to the maximum and follow the ball on its way to the teammate. The setter follows the flight of the ball with his eyes. The whole body is bent backwards passing the ball to the spiker.

Setting the Ball with One Hand Forward

Fig. 4.30: Setting the ball with one hand forward

In this way the player only sets balls that are very high and very close to the top of the net, and if the player is unable to lift it with both hands. In most cases balls, which are set in this way, allow the player to attack using a so-called "first tempo", the first time attack. This attack is almost always successful and almost no defence is good enough for it. The setter performs setting with the hand that is closer to the net. Receiving is done from the shoulder and elbow, mostly from the wrist, but the biggest weight is taken by fingers. The ball is sent to the spiker. As a rule, the interaction between setter and spiker is always a success, and the action is very attractive.

Setting the Ball with One Hand Backward (Using a Jump)

| 1 | 2 | 3 | 4 | 5 | 6 | 7 |

Fig. 4.31: Setting the ball with one hand backward (using a jump)

This is an extremely difficult but very attractive element. A perfect technique of a hand, fingers and arm, as an extremely good linking of a played combination "setter-spiker". Those are balls aimed to be accomplished as "first tempo" (or the first time attack). When performing this technique, the setter simulates or feints the block, usually these actions are very successful. In order to perform this element, the ball has to be passed very near the net and it can only be set in this way. In the jump, the player stretches out both hands as though to touch the ball with fingers. At the last minute he decides to set the ball only with one hand, behind his head, which is a double surprise for the opponent's block. The whole body participates in setting the ball (mostly the arm from shoulder, then the elbow, hands and fingers). After the setting, the player returns to his starting position .

Setting the Ball from the Back Row in a Jump Forward (Towards the Net)

Fig. 4.32: *Setting the ball from the back row in a jump forward (towards the net)*

Very often, due to strong serves and spikes, the setter is obliged to go into the court 3, 4, even 5 meters from the net, if only to save badly received balls. Then he can only send a ball toward the net for a spike. There are two basic responses in such cases:

A – first, he is supposed to do it using a jump. By doing this he is speeding up the game and disturbing the rhythm of the block. Although for some blockers it does not matter whether or not the player sets the ball with or without jump. It is generally a last minute decision whether or not to jump which generally allows the spiker to attack more successfully.

B – second thing is that the player should always be turned to the net and the player to whom this set ball was intended to be sent. In this case it is possible to exclude the surprise element on the part of the teammate, who will not know if the ball will be set for him or someone else. This way, the spiker can get a better feel for his setter. That also conditions them to establish an interaction and understanding. All other principles that apply to setters in jump forward apply here as well.

Exercises for Passing and Setting the Ball

Fig. 4.33: Exercises 1-2

Note: The Numbers on the lines of movement signify the order of exercises.

Exercises for a One-handed Set

Fig. 4.34: Exercises 1-2

Note: The Numbers on the lines of movement signify the order of exercise.

Tipping Exercises Second Ball (Setter)

Fig. 4.35: Exercises 1-2

Note: The Numbers on the lines of movement signify the order of exercise.

The Simple Low Service

| 1 | 2 | 3 | 4 | 5 | 6 | 7 |

Fig. 4.36: Simple low service

There are several types and variations of services. In the game of volleyball the following service techniques are most frequently used:

- The simple low service,
- The side tennis service,
- And the jump service.

It is necessary for beginners to start with the simple or low service. Later on, through training, they should learn all other types. During the game, the player will choose the service that will be the most convenient for him and then improve it to perfection down the line.

In the simple service, the player is turned sideways toward the net, somewhat bent forwards, and one leg is a little in front (see nos. 1, 2, 3). The player holds the ball in his left hand, lower than the waist and sets it - not very high. With hand stretched out, he hits the ball with his fist or palm. The weight of the body from the starting position is transferred from the right to the left foot (see nos. 4, 5, 6). The first aspect of the service that has to be mastered is to serve properly, once this is done the player should acquire the confidence to serve the ball and send it to certain points on the opponent's court, i.e. to serve with precision.

The Sideways Service

1   2   3   4   5   6   7   8

Fig. 4.37: Sideways Sevice

This was the type of service used in the past. Today, in modern volleyball it is not so popular. The side service has two variations, depending on the direction the ball takes when hit. In one case the ball is hit as a feint and in the other, the hit of the hand makes it waver deceptively. In both cases, the player is outside the court, standing slightly astride, towards the net. The ball is held in one hand and thrown up with it (see nos. 1, 2), while the hit is done with the other hand. The ball should be tossed into the air , but not too high, as the hit is made with practically the whole body, the weight of the body being transferred from one leg to the other and the ball is hit with the hand. In the case of feint, the hand is open (the whole ball lies in the hand). By using the arm and the body, the player tries to pull it down into the court of the opponent (see nos. 6, 7, 8), while in the case of the wavering/deceptive service, the hand is closed (fist). If the hand is opened, the hit is made with the palm, it is immediate and at the ball's highest point. The player does not follow the ball, but stands straight up.

The Overhead Serve* (Tennis Serve)

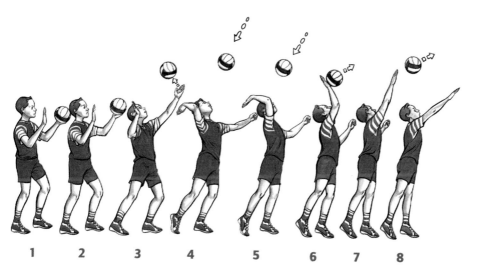

Fig. 4.38: Overhead Serve

Due to closeness of the net this service is used as a tactical service from the back line of the court, the server selects a weak spot in the opponent receiver on whom he focuses and serves the ball to. It is often served from a greater distance from the net and has a wavering or deviating trajectory. The serve is done so that the ball is set up with one hand and hit with another. The arm is stretched out as in the spike. The ball is in contact with an opened hand for only a short time and is often hit with either the palm or fist. If the fist service has been wavered/ deceptive, it makes the reception difficult for he opponent. This service can also be performed in a semi-jump, if a jump is used there will be less waive/spin on the ball, but it is quicker and stronger and often confuses the receiver, who may have to consider very quickly has to receive ball, for example with fingers or to dig as the ball flies straight in the chest level. Each player should evaluate, together with the coach, from which distance should the service be made in order to remain wavered/deviated by spin but sure as much as possible.

* Service with a deviated trajectory

The Jump Serve

Fig. 4.39: Jump serve

Today, this is the widest used service in competitive vollleyball. Players like it because it's looks so attractive. It is not so easy or sure, and its use is most frequently justified when used by masters of volleyball, where again it is best used by tall and strong players.

The name, jump serve, speaks for itself, as it is a spike, performed from outside the court, and the player sets himself up with the ball. All that goes for the element of spiking, goes for this service as well. The player rushes forward from some 4-5 meters outside the court. The ball is thrown with the same hand with which it will be served. It goes high up in the air in front of the player. The player makes two-three steps and jumps in the air, spiking into the opponent's side of the court. The jump up must be outside the court, while when the player comes to the ground he can step into his part of the court. When practicing this serve, one can start from inside the court. Slowly then the distance from the net is being enlarged (according to abilities).

Service Hit Exercises

Fig. 4.40: Exercises 1-5

Note: The Numbers on lines of movement signify the order of exercises.

The Muscles Used in the Overhead Serve (Tennis Serve)

Fig. 4.41: Muscles used in the overhead serve

1   Brachial triceps (extensors of the forearm)
2   Straight abdominal muscle (bends the body)
3   Thigh quadriceps (extends the leg below the knee)
4   Gastrocnemius – triceps muscle below the knee (foot extensor)
5   Finger extensors
6   Deltoid muscles – shoulder raisers
7   Back muscles (straightens the back)

Exercises to Develop Flexibility and Strength

Fig. 4.42: Exercises 1-10

Note: The numbers relate to each different muscle group defined on the left.

Classical Spike (Jumping up with Both Feet)

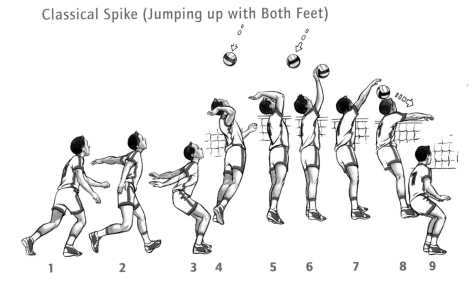

| 1 | 2 | 3 | 4 | 5 | 6 | 7 | 8 | 9 |

Fig 4.43: Classical Spike

The basic, classical spike is made, in most cases from a distance jumping with both feet, rarely with one foot. However, it is possible to play it from the spot. There are several types of spiking, depending on the position which the player takes by the net, for example left, middle, right spiker or player of the back line – diagonal spiker. Spikes also differ in accordance with the trajectory they follow, so it is possible to have a: diagonal, parallel or over the block.

There are 5 important phases in performing spike:

The run up to the net	The arm position
The jump up	The spike
The body in the air	The recovery or return to the starting position.

For players receiving the service, running to the net should begin from 3-4 meters distance, and for the players beside the net 1-2 meters, or even from the spot. The jump up should be strong and as high as possible; the body in the air should not be bend too far back. When spiking, the player should remain calm in order to observe the block and the position of opposition players. The spike itself should be performed with the whole body plus spread hands, arms, and open shoulders.

The Spike Jumping up with One Foot

Fig 4.44: The spike jumping up with one foot

The name of this element explains that the spike is being made by jumping up from one leg. The spike is not common, but is used in attack from behind the head mostly and in tactical variations. Such an attack is performed with short and low balls (penalty behind the head – first service). The spike is made only in a run-up to the net mode. The approach is made mostly with two steps, the third is for jumping up from one foot. If the left foot is used, the spike will be done with right hand and vice versa – when jumped from the right foot, the hand used will be the left one. The hand is raised high into the air the shortest way, body is slightly bent backward and spike is shot in a synchronized way: hand, arm, upper part of the body forward. The player jumps down on both feet. It is unnecessary to mention that the player follows the opponent block and formation of players on the other side.

VOLLEYBALL ABC

The Spike from the Middle of the Court (with a Turn)

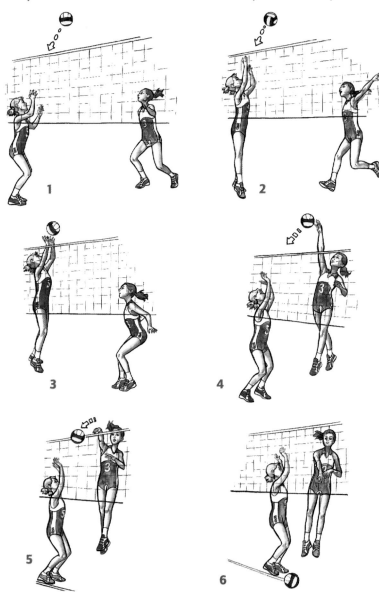

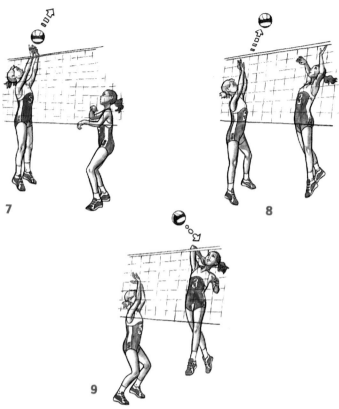

Fig. 4.45: The spike from the middle of the court (with a turn)

In most cases the spike is done from the middle of the net, and requires complete synchronization of all parts of the body. The steps, approach - running up to the net and jump, all of these movements are performed in one direction, and it is in the air when the body turns, the action results in the body being turned to the opposite direction. The spiker is directed to make the hit to the diagonal, and in the air, turning his body for 180 %, he makes the opposite diagonal. He thus avoids the block created by the opponent, and spikes mostly into the part of the court that is not defended. These spikes are very powerful and often undefended. They are straight and allow the ball to be caught at the highest point, and if the ball touches the opponent block, it almost always goes from block out of the court.

A Spike from the Shoulder, Elbow, and Hand

Fig 4.46: The spike from the shoulder, elbow, and hand

This does not differ much from the basic or classical spike, the principles of running, jumping and body position in the air are the same. The difference lies in the position of the arm and the hand when spiking. This spike is done more from the shoulder and hand and it is asymmetric, meaning that there is no complete synchronization between body and hands. When the basic spike is done correctly, the body is turned in one direction, while the arm and the hand act in another, i.e. the hit is done from the shoulder, with elbow and hand acting in the last phase of the spike, and has the objective of avoiding the block. Usually, these hits are somewhat less powerful than when both body and hands act in the same direction. As we mentioned earlier, this spike is often used to avoid the opponent's block in cases when ball has not been well set and the spiker cannot take the correct position.

Exercises to Practise the Spike

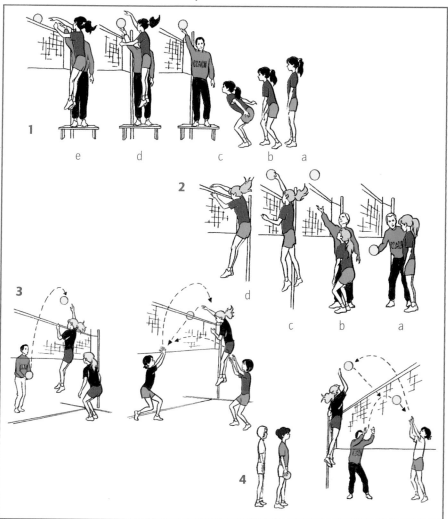

Fig. 4.47: Exercises 1-4

Note: The Numbers (or letters) on the lines of movement signify the order of exercises.

"First Tempo" ("First Time Attack")

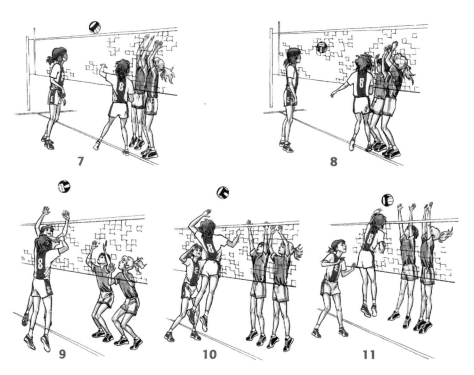

Fig. 4.48: *"First tempo" ("first time attack")*

This is usually played from the center of the net, and is the type of spiking used by middle blockers, who are, as a rule, the tallest players, whose main task is to block opponent spikers, and in certain cases, perform a quick attack. For a successful first tempo, it is necessary that a service or a ball hit by the opponent is well received. Then, the ball is passed to the setter, who must precisely set it for the spiker. The attack by first tempo or "first time attack" will be successful if the ball passed to the setter was high and close to the net. If this is the case then the setter should be able to jump and set the ball to the spiker at some half a meter from the net and in a quick action complete the attack.

A penalty is also the main means to make a so-called "second tempo". The "second tempo" has a task to distract and trick the opponent block and leave the space without block on the net, so that in the action to follow, the teammate can spike the ball. Only with feinting and first tempo can the second tempo be completed.

Second Tempo

Fig. 4.49: Second Tempo

In volleyball, like in all team sports, good cooperation is necessary., but in this technique it is vital. The middle player feigns to spike, in order to take the hit of the so-called penalty. The player feints the move of spike, attracting the opponent block to block the spike. Nevertheless, the ball is allowed to pass to the correct spiker, the player intersects with him and as a result should find himself in a situation where there is no opponent's block. If the blocker succeeds to make a block after the feinted spike, it's not usually such a good block as to stop a well aimed hit. As the point is won in 99 cases out of 100, which makes these moments in the game very efficient, This is one of the most frequently performed variations of the second tempo, and it is possible to make it work using several other variations.

Spike from the Back Row (Spike of the Diagonal Player)

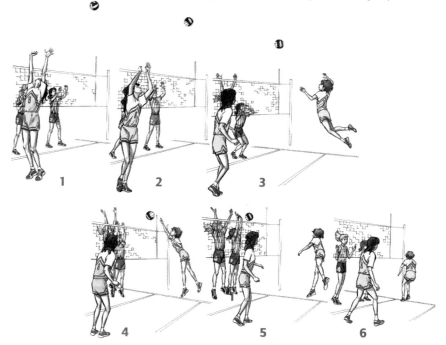

Fig 4.50: Spike from the back row

In modern volleyball, it is not sufficient to have only the front three players participate in the spike attack, the whole attack must be strong, diverse and efficient. That's why it is useful to have the back zone spiker join in the attack. The back zone spike is used from zone number one. The player performing the spike is a specialist player – a diagonal/diagonal player who, after service, immediately takes position in the zone one and from that position he is able to attack. The back-row player cannot spike and attack from the front line, but must jump from the back-row, spike the ball and after the spike must land in the three-meter zone. The back-row attack is often also performed from zone six, and sometimes from zone five. Diagonal players are those who are able to spike differently set balls, in that they have perfect coordination of the arms and body work, good jumping abilities and a sense of space. The technique of the spike is as in the basic spike, combined with all the previously described qualities of the spiker.

Muscles Used in Spiking the Ball

Fig. 4.51: Muscles used in spiking the ball

1	Deltoid muscles – shoulder raisers
2	Neck extensors
3	Gluteus – bottom muscle (hip extender)
4	Gastrocnemius – triceps muscle below the knee (foot extensor)
5	Back muscles (straightens the back)
6	Thigh quadriceps (extends the leg below the knee)
7	Oblique abdominal muscles
8	Arm lifting muscles (forward – backward)
9	Finger extensors
10	Brachial triceps (extends the forearm)

Exercises to Develop Strength and Flexibility

1. Touch your heels (5)

2. Abdominal muscles drills (7)

3. Push-ups on a bench (9/10)

4. Stretching shoulder area and back (5)

5. Jumping rope drill (4/6/8)

6. Circles with a medicine ball

7. Throwing shot-put balls from the chest (2-4 kg) (1-10)

8. Throwing sand bags overhead (1-5 kg) (1-10)

9. Climbing up the stairs (3/4/6)

10. Jumping over hurdles

Fig. 4.52: Exercises 1-10

Note: The numbers relate to each different muscle group defined on the left.

Playing the Ball from the Net with One Hand

Fig. 4.53: *Playing the ball from the net with one hand*

This is a very delicate and important moment. The player must assess, in a fraction of a second, whether he will play the "dig", with his foot or one hand. The hit is made in a quick, but careful and calm approach to the net. Balls that are hit near the top of the net, fall vertically to the ground, while those that hit the net lower, fall slower and less vertically and they're not so hard to play.

The player must approach the net at some two meters with one foot forward. Using either his right or left hand, mostly with his hand or fist, he should hit the ball sending it up in the air. It may also happen that he contacts the ball with his forearm.

The player is usually in a semi-squat and almost always falls sideways from this semi-squat position or astride position as part of his follow through. This is actually a technique that could be classed as rebounding rather than passing the ball; as such balls are quite difficult and unpredictable to read.

Playing the Ball from the Net with a "Dig"

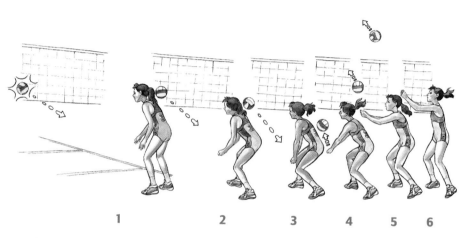

1	2	3	4	5	6

Fig. 4.54: Playing the ball from the net with a "dig"

The most important thing is that the player doesn't run rashly to the ball that bounces off the net. In order to receive the ball properly the player requires an excellent estimation of the distance of himself from the ball.

It is very important to bear in mind that the balls that hit the net lower, towards the lower line, are easier to catch, as they don't fall so quickly or as vertically to the ground, as the ones from the upper part of the net.

A calm approach to the place where the ball hits the net (some two meters) is sufficient to send the ball up in the air with a "dig", from where a teammate will be able to pass it on.

When the low "dig" is used the legs are slightly apart and squat, following the height of the ball, the arms are fully extended and the hit is made with forearms upward. At the moment of hitting the ball, hands are put together.

Playing the Ball from the Net with the Foot

Fig. 4.55: Playing the ball from the Net with the foot

The most difficult balls can only be played in this way. They are the balls that fall in the top of the net or a little lower and fall to the ground quickly and vertically. Such balls cannot be played and returned either with one hand or with a "dig". The only reason why this is the only way to save them with the foot is simple, viz the foot is closest to the ground and hence the closest body part to such balls. Two cases provide support for this statement, where blocks that are not well put together, many balls fall between the block and the net, in such an instance there is no time to bend or to play the ball with a hand or a "dig". Therefore, the player using a high level of attention and calmness, must hit the ball with the most appropriate foot – right or left. On the other hand, many balls that come into the net during the game are easy to hit with the foot, if this is the case, the player should attempt to hit the ball with the arch (instep) of the foot or even with the knee. The same principle applies here as has been mentioned previously viz. never approach the net rashly, and never get too close to it.

Hitting Balls from the Net Drills

Fig. 4.56: Exercises 1-4

Note: The Numbers on the lines of movement signify the order of exercise.

Blocking – Individual

1   **2**   **3**   **4**   **5**

Fig. 4.57: Blocking – Individual

In order to perform a successful individual or single block, it is important, first of all, to approach the net. However, if the player is deep into the court, then this blocking must not be done running toward the net. The movement is upward, parallel with the net, and following a step aside. The arms are fully extended, and bent forward at a small angle, i.e. not in line with the body. The hands are spread and relaxed. The fingers are slightly bent forward, as in the techniques of playing the ball with fingers of both hands (see Fig. 4.1). It is important to follow with the eyes the movement of the ball and the intention of the opposition player. It is also important to jump up to the block a little after the strike of the opponent's spike. When the block is individual, it should be possible to block diagonals, except when the opposition player is spiking parallel. Then it is best to jump and change the intention in the air, namely, jump as if to play parallel and then, change position of hands in the last moment for diagonal. Hands, when in the air, should be on the other side as much as possible when blocking the ball.

Double (Two-man) Block – Active

Fig. 4.58: Double (two-man) block – active

All principles valid for individual block apply for the double block. It is important to pay attention and to arrive to the net in time, to adopt the correct hands and arms positions.

The movement is parallel to the net, and hands must be raised immediately. The jump for block must be performed some time later than the spike – meaning that the spiker is allowed to jump on the opponent's side, then take over the intention and jump. In group blocks, the player that joins in must jump as in the individual block, i.e. as close to the net as possible in this way the two players make a symmetric whole. In most cases player on the end blocks parallel and the middle blocks diagonal attack, except when the tactical needs of the team demands that they have to block one or the other direction. Most often it is the diagonal blocker that should be protected, depending of course, on the opposition spiker. The most important thing is to keep the block as united and high as possible, and over on the opponent's side as much as possible. In active blocks, it is important to send the ball directly into the court of the opponent.

Double (Two-man) Block – Passive

Fig. 4.59: Double (two-man) block – passive

There is no big difference in the basic approach to this type of block. The only difference is in position of the arms. In the active block, arms and hands are as far forward as possible. The arms are spread out in order to return the ball into the court of the opponent, when hit, and as vertical as possible. In passive blocks, it is necessary to evaluate if the intention of the opponent is to take the position for attack with a powerful or tipped ball. His hit into the block would be weak, in order to have the ball return slowly to their possession. In that case, hands are straighter, so that the ball flies in a soft arch and returns to the defending team, enabling them to initiate a new attack. Passive blocks are usually unintentional, except when performed by extraordinary players who can read the game and predict the intention of the opponent, due to their extensive experience and knowledge.

As a general rule the active block should be the one most often used.

Triple (Three-man) Block - Passive

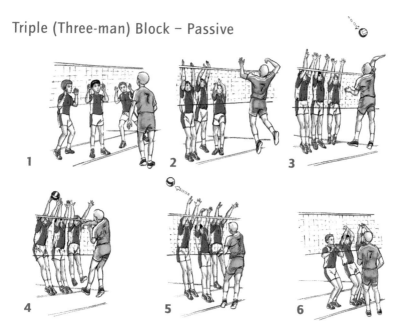

Fig. 4.60: Triple (three-man) block – passive

Whether it is a passive or an active block, the most important thing that the players always have complete concentration and the desire to block the opposition's spiker.

Remember! A good block is a good defense.

In the triple as in the single and double block, it is better to use the active one, which actually means the counterattack. Passive attack is more of a theoretical thing and is usually carried out spontaneously. In the triple block, all the basic principles apply: viz. jump up parallel to the net, no waving hands, as late as it is possible, hands over on the side of the opponent and the most important, follow closely the intention of the opponent spiker and stay calm. Three-men block is mostly formed in the center, and sometimes from the sides of the net. The middle player decides on the position, while the side players join in and make a unique whole. It is used in cases when the opponent attacks with high balls, and also medium high but long, which it is possible to block.

Pre-exercises and Exercises for Learning the Block and for Blocking

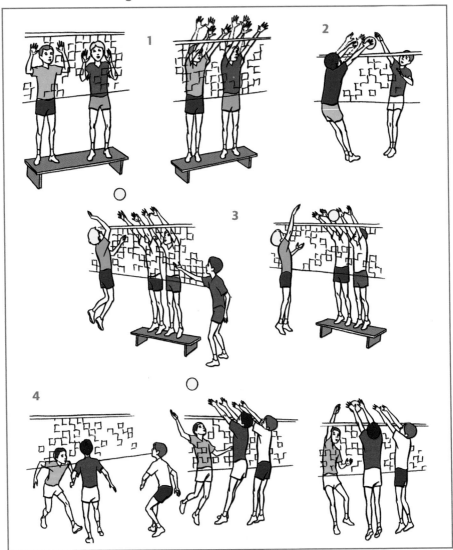

Fig. 4.61: Exercises 1-4

Tipping (Preparation Exercises without the Block)

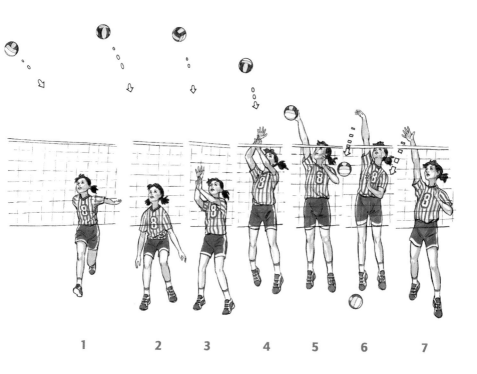

Fig. 4.62: Tipping (preparation exercises without the block)

This kind of spiking is mostly used in two cases: a) when the Spiker estimates that the opponent's block is well positioned, b) when part of the opponent's court is undefended, due to a poor player formation. Tipping has the greatest effect when the ball is placed in a specific part of the opponent's court, at some 3-4 meters from the net, which in general is the least well defended space. In this technique, the fingers are responsible for most of the work done, with the movement coming predominantly from the wrist.

Muscles Used in a Double Block

Fig. 4.63: Muscles used in a double block

1	Finger extensors
2	Deltoid muscles – shoulder extensors
3	Gluteus – bottom muscles (hip extensors)
4	Foot extensors
5	Brachial ericeps (extends the forearm)
6	Thigh quadriceps (extends the leg below the knee)

Exercises to Develop Strength and Stamina

Fig. 4.64: Exercises 1-12

Note: The numbers relate to each different muscle group defined on the left.

Tipping (Preparation Exercise with the Block)

Fig 4.65: *Tipping (preparation exercise with the block)*

This type of spike is mainly used in two cases, when the Spiker estimates that the block of the opponent is well positioned. The spiker decides to attack with a tipped ball. First he attacks when the part of the opposition field is undefended (poor formation of players), and in the second case, in case of excellent players, when the ball is so highly hit that it is impossible to avoid the block. In that case, the tipped ball from the block returns in a soft arch back to the field of the spiker or from the block (if net is close), or when it hits the block it is tipped out.

Tipping the Ball by Setter with One Hand

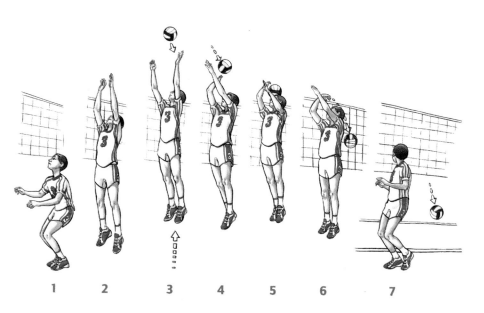

Fig. 4.66: *Tipping the ball by setter with one hand*

This is almost always used as a surprise. In the case when spikers cannot achieve an attack in a couple of attempts, due to a good block and the good delayed play of the opposing team, then the setter may decide to tip the second ball into the opponents court. In most cases such moves are successful. However, there are also cases when the ball is so well passed, so high and so close to the net that the setter has the possibility of attacking, and winning a point for the team with a tipped ball. Of course, this is used when the opposition block is very good and defensively strong. In a change of the rhythm, the tipped ball of the setter is very efficient and may have a negative impact on the opposition. Technically speaking this skill should be performed, with the hand that is closest to the net.

Tipping the Ball by Setter with the Hand Away from the Net

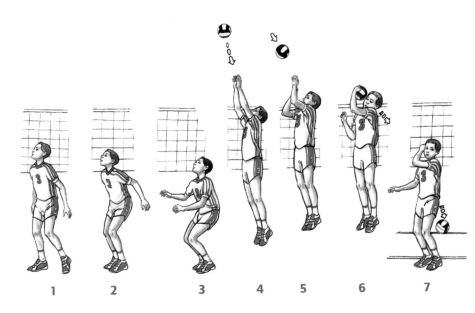

Fig. 4.67: Tipping the ball by setter with the hand away from the net

In modern volleyball the principles outlined above apply equally well to the production of this skill. In the event of the of spiker's inability to attack and win a point, the setter takes over the attacking role and brings a point to his team by tipping the ball. The moment of surprise comes in as all the attention is focused on the spiker who should hit the third and final ball, namely the spike. That is why the opponents would not expecting an attack from an setter, and the opposition defense is not concentrated on the attack from this player. The efficiency of this attack is almost 100% and very often it completely demoralizes the opposition. From the demonstration poster it is obvious that all phases are the same as in setting from a jump.

Chapter 5

TACTICAL TRAINING

Important Notice:

The section about the tactics is dedicated first of all to coaches and teachers of physical education in schools, working with younger age categories. It is important that young volleyball players and beginners should receive instructions from them.

Tactics

In volleyball as in all games, the team-tactical element is an important and complex part of the game, and is usually introduced only when all basic elements of the physical, technical and psychological, are thoroughly mastered. Tactics are best taught when the players are in good psycho-physical condition and are able to perform correctly all basic technical skills/individual tactics (for example, the receive, set, block, spike and others). The basic reason is that all these actions depend on one another and should become conditioned reflexes, thus making all parts of the game inseparable and indivisible. On the other hand, tactics/team tactics, through its systems enables, in the optimum way, the combination and connection of all individual qualities of players into a whole team.

All systems and variations in volleyball are outlined and adapted to the quality of players. Very few tactics can be attempted by a team without any good players. In other words, it is counter-productive to teach tactics to players who cannot yet reproduce a skill with any consistency.

If the players wish to benefit from the knowledge of tactics, they must be able to comply with some basic tactical principles. Not complying with these principles, by some players, diminishes the tactical value of the team and can adversely affect the results. Tactics and its systems allow the team to utilize all abilities of the player, first of all, by collective actions. The volleyball game is composed of numerous individual actions, allowed only if they are part of a game of the group. Volleyball is a team sports game. In volleyball as in no other team games there is a dependence on teammates that is extremely important.

Individual Player Tactics

As in all other sport events, tactics are important in order to accomplish success, both collectively and individually, and the same is true for volleyball. Each player, whether he spikes, blocks the service or plays within the field, is required to think tactically. For example, in volleyball, the setter is the most important element in the team's tactical thinking. Without going into further analyses, the setter is the brain of the team. It is from him that practically all attacks (except service and block) come. He evaluates, according to the height and length, to whom, when and where, he will set the ball, and, taking into account the opponent team's block, which should be avoided. The success of the attack depends on all these things. Certainly a setter must have information about the present form of the opposition spiker and to realize the importance of this point.

The Basic Types of Tactical Attacks in Volleyball

For each volleyball team it is important to know and apply three basic systems and one variation:

1. Formation of teammates when receiving the service, from which will result the position of players for the attack

2. Formation of players in defence

3. Formation of players when protecting the spiker, or receiving the ball that bounced off from the opponent's block

4. Position in the variation of tipping – by the opposition setter when he is in the front line.

For all these tasks, the selection of players must be done, first through the basic system of service receiving "everyone everything" (or 6+6)

Basic System "Everyone – Everything" (6+6)

This is the simplest and easiest way to start to teach tactics by having the beginners start to apply tactics to the receipt of service. Five players participate in the receipt with only one, the setter, being by the net. In this system, all players are in a position which, besides receiving, would also allow them, depending on the zone in which they are positioned, to set, spike or block. In other words, they may be called on to do everything, receiving services, setting, spiking, blocking, etc.

Due to the rotation order, the players change their positions clockwise, and they are obliged at some stage to be placed in all zones of the playing court. That is why in this system, they are able to do every action possible in volleyball.

This system also develops the utilitarian nature of a volleyball player and provides a chance to every player to use his strongest individual skills. There is also a chance for teachers and coaches to evaluate the possibilities and the quality of each and every player, based on which they will be able to make the right selection of players on their individual skill level.
     In order to continue on the path of specialization, the following is a good way to apply a system that is a little more complex.

From the sketch of this system (see Fig. 5.2), it is obvious that five players are in a defensive formation to receive the service at some 6-7 meters from the net, turned towards the setter who is in zone three, some two meters away from the net. The ball should be passed as high as possible to the setter, so that he can pass it on to his teammates. The illustration shows the desired direction of the ball. Each of the five players controls his part of the court. The players are never to stand in a straight line beside each other. It is always necessary to be some 10-20 centimeters away from a teammate, to the front or to the back so to avoid the simultaneous receiving of the service. Communication between the players is of key importance.

The Selection and Specialization of Players for the 4+2 System

It is necessary for beginners to make the right selection of available players. The 4+2 system is somewhat more complex than the others, but has the simplest and most purposeful formation of players two reasons:

First of all, due to its simplicity and equal participation it is the most acceptable system for insufficiently trained players.

On the other hand, this system allows for all players to master and apply all elements of the game of volleyball and, because specialization is not so strict, to be virtually au-fait with volleyball. It is specially important for setters, who in other elements are rather left out, especially in the full game, as the 5+1 system does not leave them many possibilities other than to stick to their special skill, "setting". The third thing is that through the 4+2 system, players have many more possibilities to prove their preference, and express all their skills in all elements of the volleyball game. In the 4+2 system, two setters are required. This gives more opportunity to all players to specialize for this position.

The 5+1 system, which used only one setter in the first line-up, comes at a later phase, when a higher level of experience is built up gradually, through more complex systems and variations in attack and defence and at higher competition levels.

Division of Players by their Specialization in the 4+2 System

In a 12-player team, it is necessary to have the following players:

a) four players with a good spike and good block;

c) four players who don't spike as efficiently who receive service and block well;

d) three very good setters of which one is the playmaker;

e) one libero player (player who is very good in receiving services and is good in defense and inside the field).

It is of utmost importance that each player has a minimum knowledge of each volleyball skill.

Out of four best spikers, one or two should be selected as the best in spiking from the back line, i.e. more than three meters away from the net. It is usually done from zone 1 or 6, and rarely (except in dire straits) from zone 5.

In the basic line-up, namely, in the first six in the 4+2 system, the team would be composed of the following:

a) Two main spikers, positioned diagonally
b) Two assistant spikers, also positioned diagonally, and
c) two setters in diagonal of the line-up
d) The libero would substitute the weakest players in the reception, for the service defense, mainly the key spikers.

The Selection and Specialization of Players for the 5+1 System

3 or 4 middle spikers, players who are the best blockers and spikers from the middle

a) Three or four receivers – players, who are excellent in reception, good in attack and good in block
d) Two Setters – utility players, who are excellent distributors of the ball – setting balls for receivers, very good blockers and have the personality and knowledge to lead the game
e) Two diagonal receivers, sure and good in performing the spike when 3 meters from the net. They should be good in attack on the net, good in blocking, and when necessary, able to receive service.
f) One libero, middle players in the back line, the player who often replaces spikers – His basic task is to receive well the serve and to be good within the field. In teams in which the players receiving service are excellent, there is a danger that the libero may disturb their system (he bothers and suffocates them). Additionally, the libero may also disturb a homogeneous team by entering and leaving the court. Libero players are usually not so tall, and logically, due to their physical limitations (their height), in defense they are unable to control most of the court as other taller players do. This happens mainly when they are playing in the center half position, and this is why they tend to play less well in this position than if they play the half position. The libero may also be used also as a substitute for tired players, and that is very useful for teams.

As a rule, liberos should be used mostly as a variation, and not so much as a system. This can be utilized if middle spikers are not good in receiving serves and when they play poorly in the field. The team can play even without a libero.

As a general rule the libero is strengthened in his position at the expense of a middle spiker or spiker receiver.

In this 5+1 system, the line-up is as follows:

1. two middle players – main blocker – spiker;

2. two spikers/receivers;

3. one diagonal spiker;

4. one setter;

5. one libero, playing in the back line only. N.B. The libero has no right to set the ball, nor to spike a ball higher than the net from the front line.

6. When using a diagonal formation the team is composed of middle spikers are on a diagonal line, as are receivers and also diagonally – spiker and setter.

Principles of Attacking Play

The most important thing for a good attack is to make a good first ball pass to the setter, and not to just send it away uncontrollably, whether it came from received service, from spiker or from a tip. The passed ball should be high and very near the net, if possible, so that the receiver can set it up in a jump. This allows the opponent to prepare the block, but makes it quite difficult to do so successfully. Whenever possible, the ball should be passed with fingers. In this way the pace of the play should be accelerated. The path of the ball is shorter to the setter then if it is passed using a hammer shot, but alternately the fingers give precision to the ball, enabling the setter more opportunity to trick the opponent's block.

When balls are passed accurately, the setter is enabled to accomplish almost any combination in order to attack.

There are seven basic types of set balls, related to the height and direction:

1. Is long and high, sent into the zone 4?

2. Is overhead set high but the distance is medium?

3. Is set high to the correction setter at the back line at some 3 meters from the net;

4. Is a penalty ball; lower, faster, a short way away from the face?

5. Is a penalty shot used by the players who can spring from one foot?

6. Is someone who has maintained contact higher and longer than the penalty ball?

7. Is the back line, some 3 meters away from the net in zone 6, is based the assistant setter or correction player.

Of course there are many other variations and semi-variations. However it is important that some principles are understood. If a ball is passed well to the setter (in a suitable way), then all the above types of ball can be put into effect . If it is impossible to avoid the block, then the ball should be set high, never medium, near the net, as they are the easiest to block. A high ball offers more possibilities as well as the obvious one, viz. to spike over the block. This is possible, because a block with two hands can never reach as high as the spiker can. Unfortunately this is often not understood and therefore not so often used.

Defence Tactics

Principles when Defending from Spike and "Tipping"

The basic types of defence are:

a) Reception of the service
b) Block;
c) Dig;
d) Defence of one's own block;
e) Defence from the tipping of setters.

When defending a spike or a ball from the opponent's attack, the defence players are moving usually from the back line to the net. The starting point is from 6-7 meters from the line to the net. Individual estimation of each player should depend on the position of the set ball from the opposition and the formation of the team's block. A player should position himself always beside or in between the block, while the place in the field depends on the distance of the ball from the net and the height of the ball played by the opposing spiker. In defence the player should move without running, in an unhurried pace forward-left-right.

In order to be calm even in the moment when the player has to receive the ball, he must be concentrated and move in an unhurried manner in order not to crash with the ball, which may happen if he runs to it.

Attack in the Basic System – Everyone Does Everything

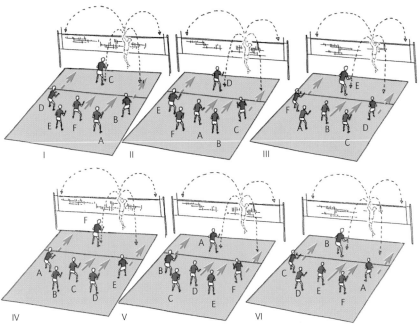

Fig. 5.1: Attack in the basic system

LEGEND

4	3	2
5	6	1

Court zones

Imaginary player

■ Front-line players
■ Back-line players

A – Aca
F – Filip
E – Egon
D – Dule
C – Cane
B – Bora

→ Direction of players from the back line – right setter from zone one and the assistant setter from zone six.

---➤ Direction of spikers from the front line: left from zone 4 and right from zone 2.

Defence in the Basic System of Service Reception – Everyone Does Everything

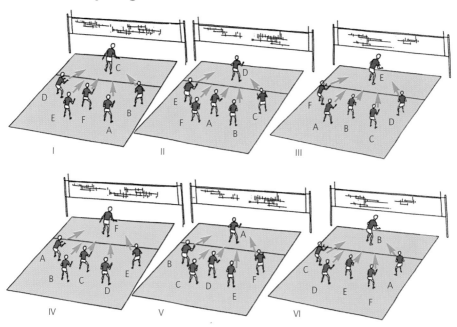

Fig. 5.2: Defence in the basic system of service reception

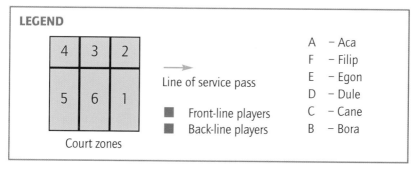

LEGEND

4	3	2
5	6	1

Court zones

→ Line of service pass

■ Front-line players
■ Back-line players

A – Aca
F – Filip
E – Egon
D – Dule
C – Cane
B – Bora

Note: In all rotations the player in zone number 3 is always the setter. All five players pass the ball – catch the opponent's serve – two from the front and three from the back line.

Attack in the 4+2 System

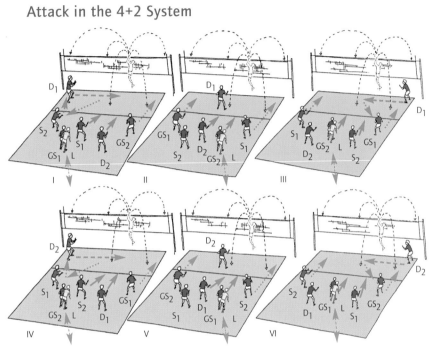

Fig. 5.3: *Attack in the 4+2 system*

LEGEND				D1	– Setter 1

LEGEND

Court zones

4	3	2
5	6	1

Imaginary player

■ Front-line players
■ Back-line players

D1 – Setter 1
S1 – Spiker 1
GS – Main spiker 1
D2 – Setter 2
S2 – Spiker 2
GS2 – Main spiker 2
L – Libero

– – – – ➤ Movement of setter at the net

———➤ Movement of spiker from the back line

············➤ Movement of front-line player away from the net

◄– – – ➤ Substitution with libero

Defence: Reception of the Serve in the 4+2 System

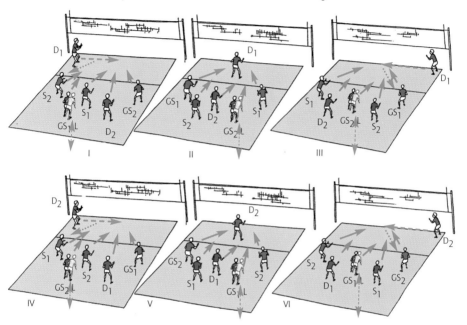

Fig. 5.4: Defence: Reception of the serve in the 4+2 system

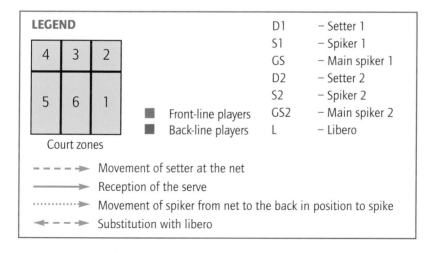

LEGEND			D1	– Setter 1
			S1	– Spiker 1
4	3	2	GS	– Main spiker 1
			D2	– Setter 2
			S2	– Spiker 2
5	6	1	GS2	– Main spiker 2

■ Front-line players   GS2 – Main spiker 2
■ Back-line players   L – Libero

Court zones

– – – – ▶   Movement of setter at the net
————▶   Reception of the serve
············▶   Movement of spiker from net to the back in position to spike
◀ – – – ▶   Substitution with libero

Attack in the 5+1System

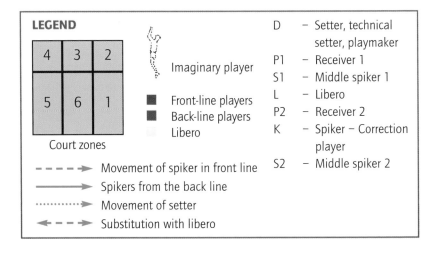

Fig. 5.5: Attack in the 5+1 system

LEGEND		

4	3	2
5	6	1

Court zones

▟ Imaginary player

■ Front-line players
■ Back-line players
□ Libero

- - - - -▶ Movement of spiker in front line

———▶ Spikers from the back line

············▶ Movement of setter

◀- - -▶ Substitution with libero

D – Setter, technical setter, playmaker
P1 – Receiver 1
S1 – Middle spiker 1
L – Libero
P2 – Receiver 2
K – Spiker – Correction player
S2 – Middle spiker 2

Defence in the 5+1 System

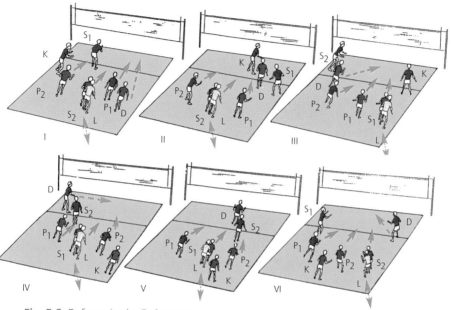

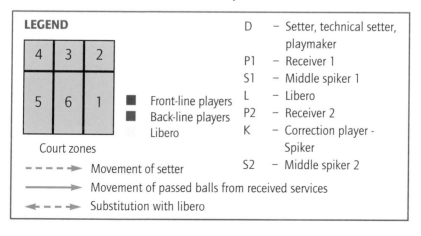

Fig. 5.6: Defence in the 5+1 system

Remark: If possible, only three players should receive the service. Spikers must remain free in order to be able to attack easily.

LEGEND					
			D	–	Setter, technical setter, playmaker
4	3	2	P1	–	Receiver 1
			S1	–	Middle spiker 1
5	6	1	■ Front-line players	L	– Libero
			■ Back-line players	P2	– Receiver 2
			Libero	K	– Correction player - Spiker
Court zones					
– – – –► Movement of setter			S2	–	Middle spiker 2
————► Movement of passed balls from received services					
◄– – –► Substitution with libero					

How to Defend against Spiking and Tipping

a) In order to defend against a spike from 6-6,5 m

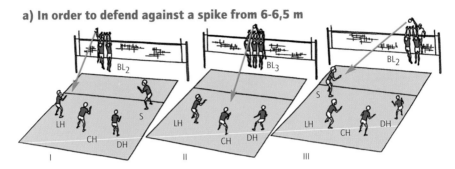

b) Defending against tipping from 4-5 m.

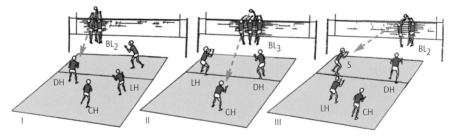

Fig. 5.7a & b: Defence against spiking and tipping

For defence it is best when the player calculates approximately where the opponent will spike, will he first spike or tip the ball. These are some features of places from which it is easiest to react when the player is in defence.

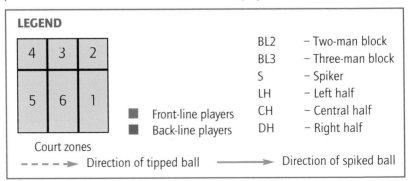

LEGEND				
			BL2	– Two-man block
4	3	2	BL3	– Three-man block
			S	– Spiker
			LH	– Left half
5	6	1	CH	– Central half
			DH	– Right half
		■ Front-line players		
		■ Back-line players		
Court zones				
- - - ➤ Direction of tipped ball		⟶ Direction of spiked ball		

How to Defend against the Block or how to Defend One's Spiker

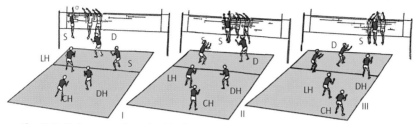

Fig. 5.8: Defence against the block

How to Defend against a Tipped Ball Placed by the Opposition Player (1 with one arm closer to the net and 2 with the arm away from the net)

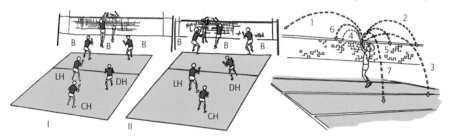

Fig. 5.9: Defence against a tipped ball

There are also seven basic types of set balls, related to the height and direction:

> Direction 1 is long and high, sent into the zone 4, 2 are overhead set high but the distance is medium; 3 is set high to the correction setter to the back line at some 3 meters from the net; 4 is penalty ball, lower, faster, short from the face; 5 is a penalty shot used by the players who can spring from one foot; 6 is somewhat higher and longer than the penalty ball. For spike that is a double point and direction 7 is the back line, some 3 meters away from the net in zone 6, for the assistant correction setter.

The efficient unflustered player can defend against all of these.

LEGEND						
			S	= Spiker	LH	= Left half
4	3	2	D	= Setter	CH	= Centre half
			B	= Players on the net\that can block	DH	= Right half
5	6	1	■	Front-line players		
			■	Back-line players	- - - ➤ Direction of tipped ball	
Court zones						

Periodisation Plan of the Yearly Training of Young Volleyball Players

Tab. 5.1:

No.	Means	Preparation period		Competition period	Transition period
		Phase I	Phase II		
1.	Exercise for improving aerobic capacity (mostly running 800-2000 m)	1/2/3/ 5/6	1/3/ 5/7	2/4/6	2/4/6
2.	Exercises for developing speed	3	3/5	3	–
3.	Exercises for developing strength with overcoming one's own weight	1/5/7	1/5/7	1/3/5	2/4/ 5/7
4.	Strength exercises with weigth load (5-8 % of the total weight of the player, lead belts, medicine balls, sand bage, rubber ropes, sand waistcoat, small barbells for older players)	1/5/7	1/5/7	1/3/5	2/4/ 5/7
5. a)	Skill and agility exercises: Basic preparation: • exercises on the ground, jumping over apparatuses, acrobatics, body exercises	3/4/7	1/2/ 4/6	2/3/ 4/5	3/5/6
b)	Specific preparation: • basic technique of playing • team, applied technique of playing	3/4/ 6/7	3/4/7	2/5	3/5/6
6. a) b)	Tactics practising the game system in attack in defence	–	1/4/7	2/4/ 5/6	–
7.	Situational training • improving adjustment to teammates • improving adjustment to opponents • improving living through irritating or obstructing situations	–	3	1/3/5	–
8.	Improving result, control	–	7	7	–
9.	Ideo-motor training: • watching movies, video taoes, cinegrams andanalyses of the same information • taping one's own technique	4	4	4	4
10.	Using specific professional literature				

Note: 1 - Monday, 2 - Tuesday ...

Useful Exercises for the General Development Of Young Volleyball Players

Fig. 5.10: Exercises 1-14

Special Exercises for Developing Jumping Abilities

Jumping is a very important ability, indispensable for the volleyball player. Exercises for developing jumping abilities should always be present in training of young volleyball players. Success in developing a good spring lies upon a right cycle of training, choice of exercises, technique of performing them and amount of exercises done and, of course, the player's genetic make up

It is necessary to develop equally the whole muscular system but primarily the area that actively participates in performing the jump.

This method of developing the body itself is divided in two parts:

1.　Development of general psycho-motor abilities and

2.　Development of specific abilities, viz the jumping skills of a volleyball player

In development of general psycho-motor abilities only the most typical ones are mentioned:

Exercises for overcoming ones own body weight, elasticity and flexibility, general agility, strength, feeling of space (jumping agility), endurance, specific strength of hip and abdomen and psychic stability (concentration).

When developing specific jumping abilities, we are talking about two phases:

In the first phase (a) development of general jumping ability, composed of mostly exercises which apply various jumping on the spot and when moving, jumps with different devices (medicine ball, small dumbbells, sand bags and lead bags, etc.), and over apparatus (spring board, beam, hurdles, or other suitable objects etc.). Then comes the use of jumping rope, sports games, acrobatics, etc.

In the second phase (b) dedicated to specific jumping skills, special attention is paid to the very technique of making the jump (run, spring, flying phase and landing).

It is important that the jump is distinguished by the flying phase. In jumping, together with the translateral movement there is also rotation. Exercises 1, 5, 6, and 10 should be performed on a softer flooring (mattress, grass, sand, etc.), at a distance of 10-30m. During the break, do the stretching and relaxation exercises. Other exercises are also done in 1-3 sets of 5-15 repeats. Break between sets is 2-5 minutes, connected with stretching and relaxation exercises.

Jumping exercises are performed throughout the year using the following stepwise action (illustrations see next page):

left   right   left

Fig. 5.11: Exercises 1-14

Acrobatics Are Very Useful and Desirable in the Formation of the Motor Apparatus of Young Volleyball Players

Acrobatics or exercises of skill and agility on the ground are some of the most important exercises that should be mastered by young players. These exercises help the player to become bolder, faster and more agile, not to mention that some of these exercises are necessary in preparations for adopting some technical training elements.

Here we have also given some additional exercises, which can help the player master the exercise itself, but with the necessary level of precaution in order to avoid injuries. With the following 12 exercises it will be possible to master the following technical elements: roll over – forward roll (2-3), and backward roll (4), flying loop (5-6) and sideways turn "cart wheel" (exercises 7-12).

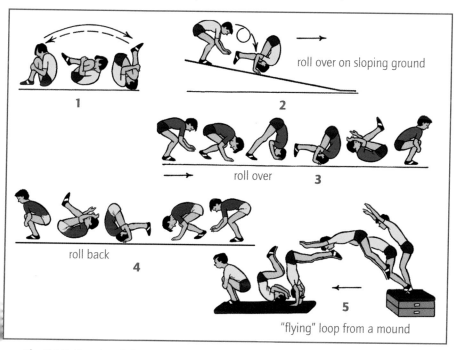

Fig. 5.12: Exercises 1-5

sideways turn "cart wheel"

Fig. 5.12: Exercises 6-13

Special Exercises for the Feet

When training and competing on various types of floor covering (wooden floor, parquet, plastic coverings, concrete, asphalt, etc.), there is an additional weight on the legs' muscular system and especially on feet. A large number of volleyball players have problems in this area. The injury and the pains that appear around Achilles tendon have already acquired a very bad name. This made many volleyball players train with less intensity, while many others had to undergo operations. The issue demands consideration and thorough analyses, so that we can to avoid these injuries and have players train as intensively as they can. Therefore, it is important that a larger part of the training is done on a good wooden floor and grass (preparation period). Changing floor during one training session without specific need should be avoided. And as prevention, dedicate significant attention to foot exercises. Some of these exercises are shown on the following pages.

The foot in itself is a masterpiece of architecture. It is composed of 26 bones, 19 muscles, some hundred ligaments and a dense construction of tendons. Most of the pain and tensions in muscles comes from insufficient flexibility, which is a consequence of uncoordinated work of muscles. That's why it is so important to exercise the feet as well, including exercising legs and feet, and why it is important to wear suitable shoes, socks and apply massage.

Another activity, which can help foot health, is to immerse them in a bowl of warm water for about 10-15 minutes. However, it is very important to make sure that they are completely dried after leaving the water. But before drying them it is an idea to walk over some brown paper and then cut carefully round the outline. By doing this periodically it will be possible have, and maintain over time, a record of the status of the feet at some specific moment in time, and will from time to time be able to make direct comparisons a precaution, what follows are a few simple exercises (see Fig. 5.14) that are easy to perform:

1   Stretch the foot forward and bring it back
2   Circle with both feet in all directions
3   Drag the feet, but with the resistance of toes on the ground

4 Pull each toe forward in the direction of longitudinal axis

5 Spread the toes, pulling the big toe to the side

6 Pick a sponge or a towel with the toes and raise it up in the air

7 Pull each toe down towards the body

8 Push back the toes with a jerk of the hand so to hear them crackle

9 Press tightly the Achilles tendon and massage it up and down

10 Squeeze, press, and twist the foot turning it in all directions to make it flexible and soft;

11 Move the brick to one side and then to the other

12 Tighten the tendon by straining the foot with the help of a belt (carefully)

13 "Charlie walk" as wide open as possible (outer edge of the foot), and then on the inside edge

14 Stretch the tendons (a), raise the heels (b), 30" each (stretching exercise)

15 Jump on tiptoes with while using a jumping rope

16 Walk alternately: on tiptoes (a), on outer edge of feet (b), on inner edge of feet (c), on heels (d) – 30" each

17 Raise the toes on a rung (espalier) as on illustration (a), and then sit on the heels (b), each 30"

18 Shower the feet using alternately warm (20") and cold water (20")

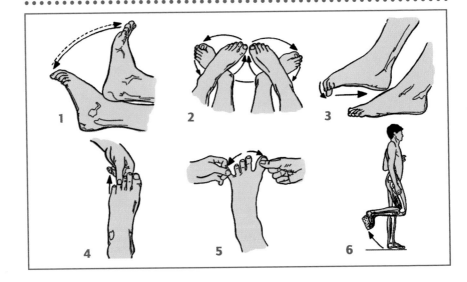

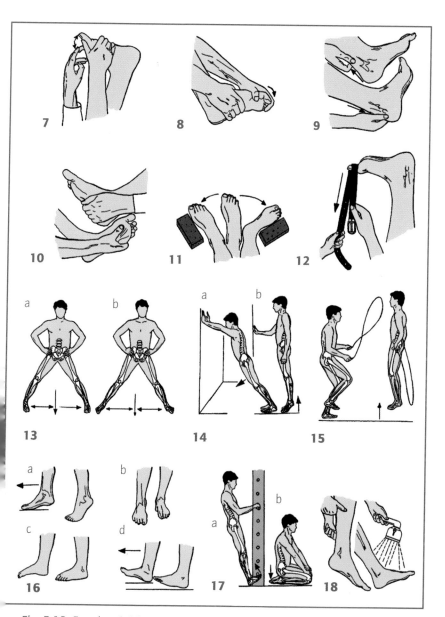

Fig. 5.13: Exercises 1-18

Control your Physical Condition by Using a Personal Pulse Meter

The best control of the effort made during training is through control of the pulse rate, which is a good and reliable method of testing an individual's level of fitness. It is well known that the number of beats per minute is very individual and that it is relatively low in young people who train regularly. It is also known that when an individual exercises the heartbeats get faster depending on the level of exertion. Therefore with more exertion the higher the pulse rate and vice-versa.

Given this, it has been possible to roughly estimate the number of heartbeats when the body is exposed to physical exertion: for example under 120 heartbeats/min when the physical exertion is medium, 120-180 when it is great and it can raise above even this when the exercise it to maximum.

By this is meant that with the help of the heart rate it is relatively easy to determine the level of a given individual's fitness, and the effort the body is exposed to during exercise. This is extremely important because in this it is possible to better determine the state of the body, improve the programme of training and follow closely effects of such training. It is also important to remember that in order to control and register such as the body weight, sleep patterns, the appetite and mood, all of which, generally, show the status of the body as a whole.

Tab. 5.2:

	Heartbeats – pulse, before and 3 minutes after exercises (number of heartbeats per minute)			
Age	Boys		Girls	
	Before exerc.	3 min. after exerc.	Before exerc.	3 min. after exerc.
7	90	120	92	124
8	87	117	90	122
9	85	115	89	121
10	84	114	88	122
11	83	113	88	124
12	82	112	87	126
13	81	112	87	126
14	80	111	86	130

All these values will change during exercise if the training is well planned. The individual will improve over time, save energy, and become efficient.

Under normal circumstances the pulse rate of girls will be a little faster than that of boys.

Number of heartbeats can best be counted in two ways:

a) Press the tip of the index on the inner part of the forearm, near to the wrist (see illustration).

b) press the tip of the index finger under the chin on the left or the right side. Count the heartbeats for 15 seconds and then multiply by four.

Making a pulse meter is easy. Prepare the following: one juice straw (a), one metal clip (b) and a piece of tape (c).

Tape all that together as shown on the illustration on the inner side of the left forearm, close to the hand. Put the forearm with the "pulse meter on a solid stable object (table would be the best) and the straw will, like a metronome, start to go from one side to the other as the heart beats, it is therefore possible to manually count her pulse rate

This is an interesting, and relatively precise instrument.

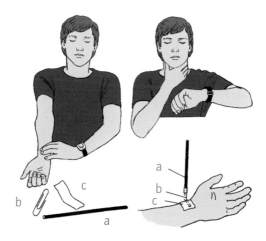

Fig. 5.14: Making a pulse meter

CHAPTER 6

So Long and Good-bye

Dear teachers/coaches

We have worked together throughout this book and I hope that you, like me, have come to love the wonderful sport of volleyball. I trust that you have acquired some useful knowledge on how your students should behave in an appropriate fashion and that they practise in order to be healthy and vital, but that above all they have a feeling of satisfaction of a job well done; which, in reality, is the purpose of young lives, and which in turn is the most beautiful period in the whole human life. We do hope that many readers will still continue to practise this wonderful sport and that some of you may become coaches to future Olympic Champions.

So long, again, and good luck in your future competitions!

BIOGRAPHY OF THE GRBIC BROTHERS

1. The Grbić brothers, the best volleyball players of Yugoslavia, were born in Klek, a village near the town of Zrenjanin. Vladimir "Vanja" was born on December 14, 1970, and the younger, Nikola, on September 6, 1973.

2. They grew up in Klek, a village in Vojvodina – Their whole childhood the brothers spent in Klek, where they were very active, together with other kids, in all that children play and enjoy. They played football, volleyball, pushed the loop and "ran after geese".

3. In 1945 the family had moved to Klek from Trebinjea, a very old historical town in Herzegovina.

4. Their father, Milos, had also grown up and learned to play volleyball in Klek. He was one of the best players in Yugoslavia and won the bronze medal in the European Championships in 1975.

5. One of the authors, Lazar Grozdanović, coached father Milos in Klek from 1971 until 1975, and he was also selector of the National Team. Laza was also coach and selector of the National Team in which the Grbić brothers played and he greatly contributed to their development.

6. The brothers learned to play volleyball in Klek with their father as their first coach and sports role model.

7. At the age of 16, Vanja joined VC Vojvodina from his original club, and some time later, his brother did the same. Vanja then joined "Mladost", Zagreb, and finally returned to play for Novi Sad. Later both brothers went to Italy where they played for the best clubs, not only in Italy but also in Europe. Vanja also spent one year playing in Brazil.

8. In 1997 Nikola Grbić, was voted best volleyball player in Europe. His subtle technique and organization of the game made the European Volleyball Confederation (CEV) proclaim him officially in 1997 the best European volleyball player of the year.

9. Vanja Grbić's hobby – fishing. When he has any, Vladimir spends his leisure time fishing. For him, it is a very useful pastime from difficult matches and trainings. And being the real sports fisherman, whenever he catches a fish, he kisses it and puts it back in the water!

10. Save Grozdanocić, the legend of Yugoslavian and Hellenic Volleyball (being both a coach and Team Selector), who also coached the brothers' father Misa, pointed out the great sports potentials of the Grbić Brothers.

11. At the Sydney Olympics Yugoslavia won the Gold medal for volleyball and it may truly be said that the brothers crowned their rich careers with Olympic Gold.

12. Vanja's popularity in the volleyball world is very great. In fact his fame has spread world wide so much that there are many clubs as far as Japan named after him.

13. As his brother Nikola before him, Vanja was officially pronounced the best volleyball player of the Year 2000. This was based on his spectacular technique, fighting spirit and the games he had played in Sydney.

Author's Biographies

Sava J. Grozdanović

One of the best coaches in Yugoslavia, born in Jelasnica near the town of Nis. He started playing volleyball in 1947 for the Belgrade club "Radnicki". The next year, the whole team went to "Zeljeznicar", where he stayed for 21 years. In 1951 he was nominated coach and selector of the National Women's Team of Yugoslavia. Until 1969 he coached at the same time several club teams: Zeleznicar (men), Partizan (women), or Red Star (women). He trained junior teams also and in 1949 won a championship title with the women's junior team of "Zeleznicar" club, with men's junior team in 1950, and in 1951, the National Women's Team of Yugoslavia, under his guiding hand, reached the 3rd place in European Championships in Paris (USSR – 1st, Poland – 2nd, and Yugoslavia – 3rd place).

1961 and 1962 he spent in Greece and invited by the Hellenic Volleyball Federation, as the first foreign coach ever, he coached Men's National Team of Greece.

In 1962, Yugoslav Volleyball Federation called him back from Greece, to take care of the Men's and Women's Teams, as the National Team Coach.

In 1969, he returned to Greece where he coached "Panathinaikos" (Men's, Women's and Junior Teams). All these teams were National Champions of Greece many times. With the Men's Team of "Panathinaikos", he reached the 2nd place in the European Cup of Cups. At the time, he was the Head Selector and Coach of the Women's National Team of Greece.

The teams Sava Grozdanovic coached won titles of National Champions of either Yugoslavia or Greece for 32 times.

Yugoslavia won gold medals in the Mediterranean Games in Naples (1963, Men) and in Tunisia (1967, Men). A bronze medal was won in the World Student Games in Budapest (1965), which was practically the European Championships.

In 1969, together with Prof. Marinkovic, he published a very famous booklet for the young "Demonstration Posters of Volleyball". He received the special "October Award of Beograd" in 1965.

Prof. Aleksandar Marinković

Professor Aleksandar Marinkovic was born in Belgrade, where he graduated at the University and Faculty of Physical Education. He was an active track and field athlete, handball player and skier (Champion of Serbia). The track and field athletes he coached achieved important results in Yugoslavia and abroad and broke 129 National and 2 European records: Nenad Stekic in long jump (8.45m – Montreal 1975) and Borislav Pisic in 60 yards hurdles (6.9 sec in Graz, 1977). Milos Srejovic was European Champion in the triple jump in Prague, 1978.

As an expert for conditioning, he coached young categories of FC Red Star Belgrade for many years. They were Champions of Yugoslavia in their respective categories. With the first team he won the Cup of Yugoslavia in 1996.

Prof. Marinkovic has written more than 30 books on physical education and sport. The books were published in 14 different languages. Among other things, in cooperation with Sava Grozdanovic, "Cinegram of Volleyball" was published in 1969. He was lecturer in numerous seminars and clinics in Yugoslavia and abroad, and he was also an international lecturer for the IAAF. For many years he was also Vice-President of the Association of Handbook Authors of Serbia. At this moment, Prof. Marinkovic teaches track and field in the Coaches College in Belgrade.

In the last couple of years he has been engaged in constructing training machines and devices to improve teaching of physical education in schools and the techniques of sports training. He holds a large number of patents.

Prof. Lazar J. Grozdanović

Born in Jelasnica, near Nis, he finished his primary school, high-school and studies at the Faculty of Philology in Belgrade.

He started his sports career in 1949 as a football player in FC Hajduk of Belgrade. He continued as a volleyball player in "Radnicki", also in Belgrade. He went to play in "Zeleznicar", and won one title of National Champion.

His coaching career commenced in VC "Crvena Zvezda" in Belgrade in 1966/67. With junior boys and senior women he twice won the National Championships.

He coached some of the best clubs in Yugoslavia: GIK "Banat" from Zrenjanin (National Champions in 1971/72), "Partizan" from Belgrade (National Champions in 1978), "Vojvodina" from Novi Sad (second place in the National Championships in 1987/88), and "Milicionar" from Belgrade (second place in the National Championships in 1999/2000).

He started working as a coach-selector of the National Team of Yugoslavia in 1972 and with small breaks he continued in this position for 28 years. In that period, the National Team won two bronze medals in European Championships (1975 and 1995), one silver medal in European Championships (1997), one bronze Olympic medal in Olympic Games 1996, and a bronze medal in the World Grand Champions Cup in Japan in 1996.

His team won the gold medal in the Universiade in Zagreb 1987, and in the Mediterranean and Balkan Games. During his involvement the Yugoslav National Team was placed first many times.

Laza was a selector for the Yugoslav National Team that won the Gold Olympic Medal in Sydney 2000.

Photo & Illustration Credits

Cover Design: Birgit Engelen
Illustrations: Vladimir Krstić
Photos: Miki Anitić

Basic Training

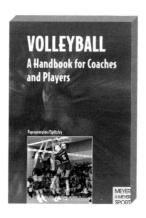

Athanasios Papageorgiou/
Willy Spitzley/
Contributor: Rainer Christ
Volleyball
A Handbook for Coaches and Players

This handbook, divided into 16 „building areas", offers a structured approach to basic training for volleyball. The manual aims at providing volleyball players with a wide range of individual-, group- and team tactical action patterns and to make the player able to exercise them as the game and the situation require. This book provides a fundamental basis for the training of specialsts to top-players.

360 pages
380 illustrations, 10 photos
Hardcover, $5^{3}/4''$ x $8^{1}/4''$
ISBN 1-84126-005-3
£ 14.95 UK/$ 19.95 US
$ 29.95 CDN/€ 22.90

MEYER
& MEYER
SPORT

MEYER & MEYER Verlag | Von-Coels-Straße 390 | D-52080 Aachen, Germany | Fax +49 (0)2 41-9 58 10-10

Expert Training

Papageorgiou/Spitzley
Handbook for
Competitive Volleyball

- Development and training of high level volleyball athletes
- How to develop an allround/ universal athlete into a specialized athlete
- Special aspects of individual, group, and team tactics

360 pages
Two-colour print
83 photos, 212 illustrations
Hardcover, 5 $3/4$" x 8 $1/4$"
ISBN: 1-84126-074-6
£ 14.95 UK/$ 19.95 US/
$ 29.95 CDN/€ 22.90

MEYER & MEYER Verlag | Von-Coels-Straße 390 | D-52080 Aachen, Germany | Fax +49(0)241-958 10-10